Mapping U. S. History with GIS

by Chris Bunin and Christine Esposito

Mapping U. S. History with GIS

ISBN 978-0-9836847-9-4

9 780983 684794 >

Table of Contents

Dedication

To three folks who helped make this work possible:

To my mother – My love for maps, adventure, and exploration began with our family vacations and has continued with your unwavering support of my dreams and aspirations.

To my friend, colleague, and mentor Dr. Robert W. Morrill for introducing me to the power of geographic inquiry! You are a GIS!

To my wife, Elizabeth for listening to me babble on and on about geospatial technologies for the past 10 years and finally saying – "just write the book already!"

~Chris

To Morgan, Julia, Kiersten and Wesley: the perfect examples of change over time.

~Christine

Acknowledgments

We would like to thank a number of people who helped make this book possible:

At Carte Diem Press: Barbaree Ash Duke, who provided guidance, templates and technical support; and Anita and Roger Palmer who tested the book's activities and deserve a big thank you for believing in publishing a book on historical GIS.

At Virginia Geographic Alliance: Coordinators Bob Morrill, Annie Evans, Joe Enedy, and Ed Kinman, the Steering Committee, and the Geospatial Technologies Committee for helping us find our way when it came to GIS curriculum development.

At ESRI: Charlie Fitzpatrick, Joseph Kerski, Tom Baker, and George Dailey who have enthusiastically shown interest and support in our historical GIS projects since the very beginning.

At LEARN NC: Andy Mink who managed "The Virginia Experiment" Teaching American History grant and saw the value in incorporating GIS into the history classroom.

At Polis Center (IUPUI) - Kevin Mickey who designed our first Historical GIS training and provided incredible support during the Virginia Experiment. You are our Mr. Miyagi.

At Newberry Library, University of Chicago: John Powell for helping us gain permission to use the Atlas of Historical County Boundaries shapefiles.

At Minnesota Population Center: Dave Van Riper for helping us make arrangements to include data and shapefiles from the National Historic GIS project.

At University of Nebraska-Lincoln: William G. Thomas III for allowing us to use his organization's most excellent shapefiles of historical railroads.

At James Madison University: Bob Kolvoord and Kathryn Keranen for helping pioneer the use of GIS in Virginia's classrooms and making this work relevant to K-12 students.

At Baruch College: Carol Berkin, who generously shared her time and expertise on the Constitutional Convention, without which the included lesson would not have been possible.

At Middlebury College: Anne Kelly Knowles whose vision and passion for historical GIS inspired many of concepts and ideas included in this work.

The instructional leaders from the "The Virginia Experiment" TAH consortium - Patricia Hughes, John Rusina, Maria Lewis, Jennifer Richter, Andrea Whitmarsh, Linda Carlton, Renee Honaker, Annie Evans, Beth Costa, and Jennifer Sublette-Williamson.

Our Fellow Teacher Scholars from "The Virginia Experiment" Teaching American History Project. Thanks to: Scott Mace, Donna Shifflett, Teresa Goodin, Robert Stewart, Jeremy Newcomb, Ann Marie Gaylord, Chris Shedd, Doug Moore, John Hobson, Stephanie Hammer, and Tamie Campbell. None of these activities would have been possible without your top notch research and dedication to creating historical GIS data sets and expeditions.

Elizabeth Bunin – This book could not have happened without your support and time holding down the NCP while we geek'd it out on ArcGIS Online!

Foreword

History can be a hard sell with children. The past seems remote from their lives, irrelevant. But as Chris Bunin and Christine Esposito show in Mapping U.S. History with GIS, the wizardry of GIS provides a wonderful antidote to this old problem.

GIS stands for Geographic Information Systems, which is a kind of computer software that enables you to combine layers of information about a place at any point in its history. You can then use GIS to ask questions about that information and get answers in the form of maps. As kids say, this is way cool. First of all, using GIS is genuinely interactive. It gets kids involved with real data – the stuff of history – as they select layers to interrogate. Second, the maps that answer their questions prompt deeper questions that go beyond dates and names. What patterns do you see, Bunin and Esposito's lessons ask, and what might explain them?

Best of all, the GIS lessons here show children how things changed over time. They will see how settlements developed in Virginia after the English established Jamestown, how the territory of the United States grew dramatically, and how Civil War battles shifted from one part of the South to another. Every geographical story raises the excellent question, "Why did certain things happen here but not there?" Your students will come to realize that geography was a puzzle the Founding Fathers had to solve while crafting the Constitution, and they will see how a clever American general used time and distance to outwit superior British forces in the final battle of the Revolutionary War. Working through these lessons, they will see history unfolding in space and time.

GIS makes history exciting by giving children the tools of revelation. I have seen GIS pull my own students into the past like nothing else. Historical information morphs into real landscapes in students' imaginations as they study the maps they have made. GIS also connects history to the digital world that students swim in today. These lessons can augment your regular textbook or launch your class on further geographical explorations of the past. However you use it, your students will gain familiarity with a powerful analytical tool, develop greater computer literacy, learn geographic concepts (such as distance, proximity, concentration, and dispersal), and find new sources of fascination in history.

Anne Kelly Knowles

Middlebury College, Vermont

Introduction: Why Use GIS in the History Classroom

He said, "I love geography!"

She said, "I hate geography!"

This was the beginning of a great partnership between Chris and Christine. Chris was working as the Director for a Teaching American History grant, and Christine was teaching US History at the same school as Chris's wife. Christine wasn't lying at the time. She really didn't like to teach geography, but she loved to teach US and World History. Fast forward 6 months from this first conversation, Chris was recruiting teachers to become part of a year-long professional development program that would teach US History teachers how to use geospatial technologies to enhance the history classroom. Christine was there. Chris was armed and ready with ArcMap and a few United States data sets (Rivers and States). Once he demonstrated how GIS can make patterns light up on the map, Christine was hooked. A year later, Christine had mapped the Constitutional Convention vote-by-vote, while Chris had mapped the evolution of Virginia's counties. From this point forward we will write in first person☺. You get the point – GIS is a game changer for helping bring geographic thinking into the history classroom.

"Why use GIS to teach US History," you ask? The better question is, "Why not?"

Do you feel the pressures of teaching a standards-based curriculum? You need GIS! GIS allows you to dynamically teach events from a variety of scales. For example, 6th grade students in Virginia public schools need to know 5 major Civil War battles. With GIS you can filter the information to show how these five battles (Bull Run, Antietam, Gettysburg, Vicksburg, and Appomattox Courthouse) were part of a collection of 360+ battles that occurred between 861-1865. You may also want to show students that the war wasn't about Lee chasing Grant, or Grant chasing Lee. Quickly filter the map based on which general was present as each battle and you can show students that Lee was in Virginia in 1861 and Grant was in Missouri...hardly a chase.

Do you ever have difficulty teaching students the interplay between geography and history? With GIS this interplay becomes obvious. Let's look at the Louisiana Purchase. Most teachers explain to students that New Orleans controlled the trade between the Atlantic Ocean and the Mississippi River System; therefore, President Jefferson felt the city and the Gulf Coast was vital to American economic interests. That sounds pretty good, but are students really able to comprehend what this means? When teaching this concept with GIS, simply start with a GIS map that contains layered data of New Orleans, major US Rivers, and current US states. First show them the location of New Orleans, and then use GIS to highlight the Mississippi River. Select the Mississippi River System. Next conduct some very simply spatial analysis, ask the map to show all of the US States that intersect a river that is part of the Mississippi River System. When over half of the United States becomes highlighted, students typically say, "Whoa!" We then ask them to explain why Thomas Jefferson wanted to buy New Orleans and the answers nearly always explain the interactions between the city, the river, and the land/states drained by the Mississippi River system.

Lastly, GIS is fun! This is a technology that our students are using with their smart phones, online mapping tools, and with gaming. If nothing else, these lessons will teach your students a critical 21st Century skill, while also learning how US history didn't happen in a vacuum.

So what's in this book? The lesson plans in this book leverage a number of data sets and lesson ideas that we developed alongside a number of other central Virginia teachers during the 2007-2008 academic year. These teachers were part of "The Virginia Experiment" Teaching American History Grant awarded to Albemarle, Charlottesville, Greene, Madison, and Orange school divisions. Each of us learned how to use GIS and then researched, designed, and created a best-practice GIS investigation. The topics ranged from the first English Colonies to the American Civil War to Jim Crow legislation. The group created data sets that shares America's story in a unique and powerful manner. We owe a lot of own our understandings and successes with GIS to this bumpy, yet exciting journey; therefore, we would like to thank the following individuals for helping build a collection of authentic historical GIS resources - Donna Shifflett (Mapping the American Revolution), Chris Shedd (Mapping the Underground Railroad), Scott Mace (Querying the Reach of Jim Crow), Stephanie Hammer (World War II Alliances), Jeremy Newcomb and Robert Stewart (GIS and the Civil War), John Hobson (GIS and Political Campaigns), Teresa Goodin (Overland Trails), Ann Marie Gaylord (Slavery: North Vs. South), Tami Campbell (Mapping the Presidential Primaries), Kevin Mickey (GISP, The Polis Center, IUPUI), and Andy Mink (Project Manager, LEARN NC, UNC-CH).

Our intent from the beginning was to create a book that you can use. The GIS maps and lessons contained here meet the realities of your classroom. The maps are created and ready go! All you have to do is log into www.arcgis.com and you are ready to "get mappy with it." Each activity (fingers crossed) is designed to be completed in 45 minutes or less and tasks students with using a variety of GIS, historical inquiry, and spatial thinking skills.

We hope you have as much fun using and adapting these lessons in your class as we have in ours.

Happy Mapping!

Chris Bunin and Christine Esposito

National Geography Standards

		Chapter Number:	1	2	3	4	5	6	7
1	How to use maps and other geographic representations, geospatial technologies, and spatial thinking to understand and communicate information		X	X	X	X	X	X	X
3	How to analyze the spatial organization of people, places, and environments on Earth's surface		X	X	X	X	X	X	X
4	The physical and human characteristics of places		X	X	X	X	X	X	X
5	That people create regions to interpret Earth's complexity		X			X		X	
6	How culture and experience influence people's perceptions of places and regions		X		X			X	
9	The characteristics, distribution, and migration of human populations on Earth's surface.		X					X	
11	The patterns and networks of economic interdependence on Earth's surface				X		X	X	
12	The processes, patterns, and functions of human settlement		X		X		X	X	
15	How physical systems affect human systems				X				
17	How to apply geography to interpret the past		X	X	X	X	X	X	X

Common Core Literacy Standards

		Chapter Number:	1	2	3	4	5	6	7
CCSS.ELA-Literacy.RH.6-8.1	Cite specific textual evidence to support analysis of primary and secondary sources.					X		X	
CCSS.ELA-Literacy.RH.6-8.2	Determine the central ideas or information of a primary or secondary source; provide an accurate summary of the source distinct from prior knowledge or opinions.					X		X	
CCSS.ELA-Literacy.RH.6-8.7	Integrate visual information (e.g., in charts, graphs, photographs, videos, or maps) with other information in print and digital texts.			X	X	X		X	X

National History Standards

Chapter Number:	1	2	3	4	5	6	7
Era 1 **Three Worlds Meet** **(Beginnings to 1620)** — Standard 2: How early European exploration and colonization resulted in cultural and ecological interactions among previously unconnected peoples	X						
Era 3 **Revolution and the New Nation (1754-1820s)** — Standard 1: The causes of the American Revolution, the ideas and interests involved in forging the revolutionary movement, and the reasons for the American victory		X					
Standard 2: The impact of the American Revolution on politics, economy, and society			X				
Standard 3: The institutions and practices of government created during the Revolution and how they were revised between 1787 and 1815 to create the foundation of the American political system based on the U.S. Constitution and the Bill of Rights			X				
Era 4 **Expansion and Reform (1801-1861)** — Standard 1: United States territorial expansion between 1801 and 1861, and how it affected relations with external powers and Native Americans				X			
Standard 2: How the industrial revolution, increasing immigration, the rapid expansion of slavery, and the westward movement changed the lives of Americans and led toward regional tensions					X	X	
Standard 4: The sources and character of cultural, religious, and social reform movements in the antebellum period						X	
Era 5 **Civil War and Reconstruction (1850-1877)** — Standard 1: The causes of the Civil War						X	
Standard 2: The course and character of the Civil War and its effects on the American people							X

Chapter 1: From London to the Fall Line – Jamestown and America's First Counties

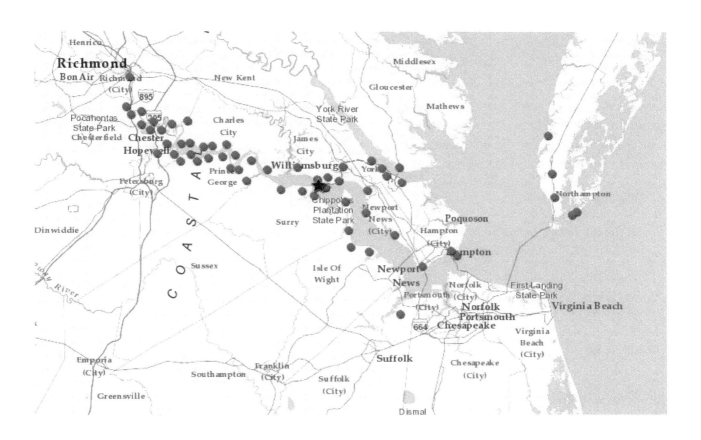

From London to the Fall Line: Jamestown and America's First Counties

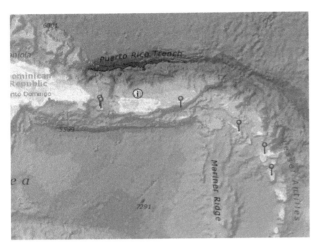

Introduction

Founded in 1607, Jamestown marked the beginning of permanent English settlement in the New World. This module is divided into two activities. "Not to be opened until...Virginia!" provides students with an opportunity to interact with key stops along the Virginia Company's voyage from London to the shores of North America and the James River. In addition to analyzing the geography of the voyage, students will also read and answer questions about excerpts from Captain John Smith's "The Proceedings and Accidents of the English Colony in Virginia," written in 1612.

The second lesson, "Why Counties?" explores one of America's many cultural inheritances from England and an unintended consequence of settling Jamestown– counties! Students use ArcGIS Online to calculate the travel time some of Virginia's early settlers faced to reach Jamestown, describe some of the reasons for creating the first counties, and identify and explain some of the unique boundaries, shapes, and names given to Virginia's counties.

Teacher Information

Time
- Activity One – Not to be Opened Until...Virginia - 30 minutes
- Activity Two – Why Counties? 30 minutes

Subjects
United States History, Geography

Level
Grades 5-12

Objectives
Students will be able to:
- Identify key segments of the Virginia Company's voyage from England to the New World.
- Read excerpts from John Smith's and answer guided questions
- Describe the relative location of Jamestown, Virginia from a local, regional, and global perspective.
- Describe the early settlement patterns of the settlers of Jamestown in 1624 and 1634.
- Use the measuring tool to calculate the time that it would take some of the Jamestown's earliest settlers to travel to Jamestown.
- Observe and describe how Virginia's counties were created from 1634 – 1890.

Spatial Thinking Fundamentals/Themes
- Location – location of key stops for the Virginia Company's voyage across the Atlantic
- Region – Virginia, Eastern North America, and East Coast of Virginia.

- Patterns – location of early settlement patterns, and the location and naming of Virginia's counties.
- Comparison – comparing Virginia's first counties to its later counties.
- Distance – measuring the distance of the Virginia Company's journey to the New World.

Extensions

- Have students explore the documents and interactive maps available at www.virtualjamestown.org to learn about individual stories and experiences.
- Research the early history of some of the counties in their own state. Research findings could include: date of creation, reason for creation, description boundary changes, origin of name, and lingering questions. Shapefiles are available at the University of Minnesota's National Historical GIS database www.nhgis.org.
- Have students look at a current population map of their own state. Locate places where new counties might be needed. Have them create and justify the names for five new counties.

"Not to be opened until...Virginia!" - Instructions

Part I: London, England

1. Go to http://www.gisetc.com/mushago. Open the map, **London to Fall Line**.
2. In front of you is a map of the North Atlantic Ocean and place marks that indicate key locations of the Virginia Company's voyage to the shores of North America. Let's take a few minutes to learn a little more about this voyage.
3. Click on **Bookmarks** and choose **London, England**. The Virginia Company was a joint-stock company based in England that sponsored the voyage to Virginia. Let's find out when and where the voyage began. **Click** on the **orange placemark** and **answer question 1 on your answer sheet.**

   Q1. In which part of London did the journey begin? What date did they depart London?

4. Close the place mark pop-up window and find the primary source **map note** ⓘ. Within this map note is an excerpt from Captain John Smith's account of the voyage. **Read the excerpt and answer question 2- 4 on your answer sheet.**

   Q2. How many ships did the company provide for the journey? How much did each ship weigh?
   Q3. Who was placed in charge of the voyage? Why was he chosen to the lead the crew?
   Q4. What was placed in a box and sealed until the group reached Virginia?

Part II: The First Stop

1. Close the map note window and then select the next Bookmark, "The First Stop".
2. The map on your screen shows two place marks – where the voyage began and the crew's first stop. **Click the information in the place mark and the primary source map note located off the coast of Africa to answer questions 5-6 on your answer sheet.**

   Q5. Where was the crew's first stop? When did they arrive to this location?
   Q6. According to John Smith's account what was the purpose of stopping at this island?

3. Next use the **measure tool** to measure the number of miles the crew sailed to reach this island. Make sure that your measurement doesn't cross any major landforms, they were sailing. **Answer question 7 on your answer sheet.**

   Q7. How many miles did the crew travel from London to reach their first stop?

Part III: Crossing the Atlantic

1. Close any place mark or map note windows and then select the next Bookmark, "Crossing the Atlantic".

2. The map on your screen shows the crew's journey. Find the cluster of placemarks on the western side of the Atlantic Ocean. Use these placemarks to answer question 8 on your answer sheet.

   Q8. What are the names of three of the locations the crew made stops in this region during the voyage? Record the name of the island and the date that the crew arrived at each location.

3. Find the primary **source map note.** Within this map note is another excerpt from Captain John Smith's account of the voyage. **Read the excerpt and answer questions 9-10 on your answer sheet.**

     Q9.   How many weeks did the crew spend in these islands?

     Q10.   How did the crew cook their food while in Guadalupe?

     Q11.   What were some of the types of animals the crew ate while on these islands? Identify three different types of animals?

4. Use the **measure tool** to answer question 12 on your answer sheet.

     Q12.   How many miles had the crew traveled up to this point in their journey?

Part IV: The Landing

1. Close any placemark or map note window and then select the next Bookmark, "The Landing".

The map on the screen shows final two stops of the journey. Use these placemarks to answer questions 13 - 14 on your answer sheet.

     Q13.   What are the names of the final two stops of the journey?

     Q14.   What was the date that the crew reached Jamestown?

2. Find the primary source **map note** ⓘ. Within this map note is another excerpt from Captain John Smith's account of the voyage. **Read the excerpt and answer question 15 - 17 on your answer sheet.**

     Q15.   What happened to some of the members of the crew on the first day that they made landfall?

     Q16.   Briefly summarize the orders that were contained in the box?

     Q17.   Who was selected to the First President of Jamestown?

3. Use the **measure tool** to answer question 12 on your answer sheet.

     Q18.   How many total miles did the crew travel up to reach Jamestown?

     Q19.   Approximately how many months did the journey take?

Part IV: Bringing it All Together

1. Using all of the different bookmarked views or the zoom tool, answer question 20 on your answer sheet. Describe the relative location of Jamestown. If you'd like you can describe at both the local (The Landing) and the region (Full Extent) level.

     Q20.   Where was the first permanent English settlement located?

Name: _____ Date: _____ Class: _____

"Not To Be Opened Until…Virginia!" – Student Answer Sheet
Directions: Use the ArcGIS Online map, "From London to the Fall Line" to answer these questions.

London, England

1. In which part of London did the journey begin? What date did they depart, London?

LOCATION	DATE

2. How many ships did the company provide for the journey? How much did each ship weigh?

3. Who was placed in charge of the voyage? Why was he chosen to the lead the crew?

4. What information was placed in a box and sealed until the group reached Virginia?

The First Stop

5. Where was the crew's first stop? When did they arrive to this location?

LOCATION	DATE

6. According to John Smith's account what was the purpose of stopping at this island?

7. How many miles did the crew travel from London to reach their first stop?

Crossing the Atlantic

8. What are the names of three of the stops the crew made in this area? Record the name of the island and the date that the crew arrived at each of these stops.

LOCATION	DATE
1.	
2.	
3.	

9. How many weeks did the crew spend in these islands?

10. How did the crew cook their food while in Guadalupe?

11. What were some of the different types of animals the crew ate while on these islands?

12. How many miles had the crew traveled up to this point in their journey?

The Landing

13. What are the names of the final two stops of the journey?

14. What was the date that the crew reached Jamestown?

15. What happened to some of the members of the crew on the first day that they made landfall?

16. Briefly summarize the orders that were contained in the box.

17. Who was selected to be the first President of Jamestown?

18. How many total miles did the crew travel up to reach Jamestown?

19. Approximately how many months did the journey take?

Bringing it All Together

20. Where was the first permanent English settlement located?

"Not To Be Opened Until...Virginia!" Answer Key

London, England
1. In which part of London did the journey begin? What date did they depart, London?

LOCATION	DATE
Blackwall	**December 20, 1606**

2. How many ships did the company provide for the journey? How much did each ship weigh? **Three; 100 tons, 40 tons, and 20 tons**.
3. Who was placed in charge of the voyage? Why was he chosen to the lead the crew? **Christopher Newport; Mariner with experience in the Western parts of the Atlantic Ocean**.
4. What information was placed in a box and sealed until the group reached Virginia? **Orders for the government**

The First Stop
5. Where was the crew's first stop? When did they arrive to this location?

LOCATION	DATE
Canary Islands	**February 18, 1607**

6. According to John Smith's account what was the purpose of stopping at this island? **To get water**
7. How many miles did the crew travel from London to reach their first stop? **~ 2000 miles**

Crossing the Atlantic
8. What are the names of three of the stops the crew made in this area? Record the name of the island and the date that the crew arrived at each of these stops. **Answers will vary**
9. How many weeks did the crew spend in these islands? **Three weeks**
10. How did the crew cook their food while in Guadalupe? **The hot springs**
11. What were some of the different types of animals the crew ate while on these islands? **Crocodile, tortoise, parrots, fish, pelicans**
12. How many miles had the crew traveled up to this point in their journey? **~5500 miles**

The Landing
13. What are the names of the final two stops of the journey? **Cape Henry, Jamestown**
14. What was the date that the crew reached Jamestown? **May 13, 1607**
15. What happened to some of the members of the crew on the first day that they made landfall? **Assaulted by Native Americans**
16. Briefly summarize the orders that were contained in the box. **The council was named and they were to elect a President to serve one year.**
17. Who was selected to be the first President of Jamestown? **Mr. Wingfield**
18. How many total miles did the crew travel up to reach Jamestown? 7100 – 7150 miles
19. Approximately how many months did the journey take? **6 months**

Bringing it All Together
20. Where was the first permanent English settlement located? **Answers will vary. Possible answers should include: Along the James River; in present-day Virginia near the Atlantic coast; in North America along the Atlantic Ocean.**

Why Counties? - Instructions

Part I: Jamestown, 1607 - 1634

1. Go to http://gisetc.com/mushago. Open the map, **Why Counties**. Click **Modify Map**.
2. The map on the screen has one star in the middle representing Jamestown, Virginia. **Click on the star and answer question 1 on your answer sheet.**

   Q1. **When was Jamestown founded?**

3. Click **Show Content of Map** button. **Turn on ☑ 1607-1634 settlements**. Each dot on the map represents a settlement that was founded between 1607 and 1634. **Use these layers to answer questions 2 – 3 on the answer sheet.**

   Q2. **What settlement patterns do you notice on this map? Where were people settling? Not settling?**

   Q3. **What are the names of some of the settlements?**

According to the original charter of Jamestown the only court for the colony would be located at the Jamestown Fort (the star on your map). That meant that if any settler was ordered to court, which happened from time to time, they were to report to Jamestown. During the early 17th century the fastest most people could travel was 2 miles per hour. Let's find out how long it would take for a few of Virginia's earliest settlers to get to Jamestown when they needed to go to court. To do this you will choose a few settlements and then use the measure tool to find out how far they lived from Jamestown. You will then do a few simple calculations.

4. Click on one of the settlements on the map. Next use the measure tool to measure how many miles that this place was located from Jamestown. Then calculate how many hours it would take for someone from that settlement to reach Jamestown. *Hint: Time = Distance divided by miles per hour*

5. **Record your answers in the chart provided with question 4 on your answer sheet.**

   Q4. **How far did some of the settlers live from Jamestown? How long would it take them to travel to Jamestown?**

6. Now find a few of the settlements that were located farthest from Jamestown. Identify the names of these settlements and calculate their distance and travel time to Jamestown. **Record this information to complete question 5 on your answer sheet.**

   Q5. **Which settlements were located farthest from Jamestown? What was their distance and travel time from Jamestown?**

Part II: Jamestown, We have a Problem!

Jamestown's court was overwhelmed due to the number of people it served. Additionally, many settlers were unhappy with the distance they needed to travel every time they had to attend court. In 1634, the House of Burgesses (the first elected assembly in the New World) created eight new courts to help relieve the overwhelmed courts. They also had to decide which settlers would report to each of these courts. They decided to follow England's model and create shires (counties). Depending on the county someone lived in determined which court they would attend. The formula was very much like building new schools and school districts today. If a school becomes full, a new one is built and school districts are redrawn to determine which students will attend the new school and which students will attend the old school.

Use the information you have just read to answer question 6 on your answer sheet.

Q6.   Why did the House of Burgesses create the first shires (counties) in Virginia in 1634?

Virginia's Counties – 1634 – 1890
Virginia 1634

7. Let's take a look at the first counties that were created. **Turn on ☑ the layer, Virginia Counties 1634**. Click on the **More Options icon** below the layer name and choose **Zoom to.** Show the table for this layer by clicking on the **name of the layer** and then clicking the **Show Table icon.**

Find question 7 on your answer sheet and record some observations about the first counties created in 1634.

Q7.   What do you notice about the location of the counties, their shapes, and their boundaries? What are the names of the new counties? What is the root/origin of the name for these counties?

Record your observations and possible explanations on the answer sheet for question 7.

Virginia 1700

8. As people continued to come to Virginia, new counties were created and named. Let's look at the new counties that were created between 1634 -1700. **Turn on ☑ the layer, Virginia Counties 1700**. Make all of the other layers except for Jamestown invisible. **Zoom to the layer, Virginia Counties 1700.** Use this map to note some of your observations about this map. Where were the new counties created? Do any boundaries or specific counties stand out? **Record this information in the table for question 7.**

9. Next, filter the layer Virginia Counties, 1700 to show only the new counties that were created from 1634 – 1700. To do this click on the **name of the layer** and **click** the **Filter icon**. Create a filter that displays features in the layer that meet the following expression: **NEW_1700 is Yes.**

10. Choose **Apply** and **Show the Table** for the filtered results by clicking on the **Show Table icon.** Use this information to make more observations about Virginia's counties in 1700. Consider the

question, what were counties being named after from 1634 – 1700? **Record this information in the table for row, 1700.**

11. Take a few moments to record any explanations or questions you have about the new counties that were created or removed.

12. **Clear any filters.** To do this click on the name of the layer and click the **Filter icon**. Then click **Remove Filter.**

Virginia 1750

13. People continued to move to Virginia and more and more counties were created. Let's now take a look at the new counties that were created from 1701 - 1750. Turn on ☑ the layer, Virginia Counties 1750. Make sure all other layers except Jamestown are invisible. **Zoom to the layer, Virginia 1750.** Use this map to note some of your observations about this map. Where were the new counties created? Do any boundaries or specific counties stand out? Which ones? **Record this information in the table for question 7.**

14. Next, filter the layer Virginia Counties 1750 to show only the new counties that were created from 1701 – 1750. To do this click on the layer you are working with and **click** the **Filter icon**. Create a filter that displays features in the layer that meet the following expression: **NEW_1750 is Yes**

15. Choose **Apply** and **Show the Table** for the filtered results by clicking on the **Show Table icon**. Use this information to make more observations about Virginia's counties in 1750. Consider the question - what were counties being named after from 1701 - 1750? **Record this information in the table for row, 1750.**

16. Take a few moments to record any explanations or questions you have about the patterns you see in this map.

17. **Clear any filters.** To do this click on the name of the layer and click the **Filter icon. Choose Remove Filter.**

Virginia 1780

18. *In July, 1776 Virginia united with the other English colonies and declared their independence from Great Britain.* Let's now take a look at the counties that were created from 1751 - 1780.

   Turn on ☑ the layer, **Virginia Counties 1780**. Make sure layer all other layers except for Jamestown are invisible. **Zoom to the layer Virginia 1780.** Use this map to make some observations about Virginia's counties in 1780. Where were the new counties created? Do any boundaries or specific counties stand out? Which ones? **Record this information in the table for question 7.**

19. Next, filter the layer Virginia Counties, 1780 to show only the new counties that were created from 1751 – 1780. To do this click on the layer you are working with and **click** the **Filter icon.**

Create a filter that displays features in the layer that meet the following expression: **NEW_1780 is Yes.**

20. Choose **Apply** and **Show the Table** for the filtered results by clicking on the **Show Table icon**. Use this information to make more observations about Virginia's counties in 1780. Consider the question - What were counties being named from 1751 - 1780? **Record this information in the table for row, 1780.**

21. Take a few moments to record any explanations or questions you have about the patterns you see in this map.

22. **Clear any filters.** To do this click on the name of the layer and click the **Filter icon. Choose Remove Filter.**

Virginia 1790

The American Revolutionary War ended in 1783 and Virginia gave control of Illinois County (The Northwest Territory) to the United States Government. Let's take a look at the counties that were created between 1781 and 1790.

23. Turn on the layer, Virginia Counties 1790. Make sure layer Virginia all of the other layers except for Jamestown are invisible. **Zoom to the layer Virginia, 1790.** Use this map to make some observations about what Virginia looked like in 1790. Where were the new counties created? Do any boundaries or specific counties stand out? Which ones?
Record this information in the table for question 7.

24. Next, **filter** the layer Virginia Counties, 1790 to show only the new counties that were created between 1781 and 1790. To do this click on the layer you are working with and **click** the **Filter icon. Create a filter** that displays features in the layer that meet the following expression: **NEW_1790 is Yes**

25. Choose **Apply** and **Show the Table** for the filtered results by clicking on the **Show Table icon**. Use this information to make more observations about Virginia's counties in 1790. Consider the question - What were the counties being named after between 1781 and 1790? **Record this information in the table for row, 1790.**

26. Take a few moments to record any explanations or questions you have about the patterns you noticed in this layer or table.

27. **Clear any filters.** To do this click on the name of the layer and click the **Filter icon. Choose Remove Filter.**

Virginia 1860

Let's now take a look at the counties that were created in Virginia between 1791 and 1860.

28. Turn on the layer, Virginia Counties, 1860. Make sure all of the other layers except for Jamestown are invisible. **Zoom to the layer Virginia, 1860.** Use this map to make some observations about what Virginia looked like in 1860. Where were the new counties created? Are any counties no longer part of Virginia? Do any boundaries or specific counties stand out? Which ones? **Record this information in the table for question 7.**

29. Next, filter the layer Virginia Counties, 1860 to show only the new counties that were created from 1791 - 1860. To do this click on the layer you are working with and **click** the **Filter icon.** Create a filter that displays features in the layer that meet the following expression: **NEW_1860 is Yes,**

30. Choose **Apply** and **Show the Table** for the filtered results by clicking on the **Show Table icon.** Use this information to make more observations about Virginia's counties in 1860. Consider the question - What were the counties being named after from 1791 - 1860? **Record this information in the table for row, 1860.**

31. Take a few moments to record any explanations or questions you have about the patterns you noticed in this layer or table.

32. **Clear any filters.** To do this click on the name of the layer and click the **Filter icon. Choose Remove Filter.**

Toponym Analysis

Toponymy is the study of place names (toponyms), their origins, and meanings. You have pretty much been doing this for each step in this lesson.

33. Your next layer looks at the origin of county names in Virginia and West Virginia based on the counties of 1860. Let's give Virginia County toponyms a geographic eye by turning on the **Toponyms Layer.** Click on the **name of the layer** and **choose the show legend icon.** Quickly look at this map. Use this information to make some observations about Virginia toponyms. **Record this information in the table for row, Toponyms.**

34. Take a few moments to record any explanations or questions you have about the patterns you noticed in this layer or table.

Virginia 1890

35. **Let's now take a look at the counties that were created in Virginia from 1861 - 1890.** Turn on the layer, Virginia Counties, 1890. Make sure all of the other layers except for Jamestown are invisible. **Zoom to the layer Virginia, 1890.** Use this map to make some observations about what Virginia looked like in 1890. Where were the new counties created? Are any counties no longer part of Virginia? Do any boundaries or specific counties stand out? Which ones? **Record this information in the table for question 7.**

36. Next, filter the layer Virginia Counties, 1890 to show only the new counties that were created between 1861 and 1890. To do this click on the layer you are working with and **click** the **Filter**

icon. Create a filter that displays features in the layer that meet the following expression: **NEW_1890 is Yes**

37. Choose **Apply** and **Show the Table** for the filtered results by clicking the **Show Table icon.** Use this information to make more observations about Virginia's counties in 1890. Consider the question - What were counties being named after between 1861 and 1890? **Record this information in the table for row, 1890.**

38. Take a few moments to record any explanations or questions you have about the patterns you noticed in this layer or table.

39. **Clear any filters.** To do this click on the name of the layer and click the **Filter icon. Choose Remove Filter.**

Bringing it All Together

40. During this activity you explored the reason for creating counties in America and then how Virginia evolved and devolved between 1634 and 1890. Finish up this activity by writing out five facts that you learned about America's first counties and/or Virginia's county creation process. Record this information under question 8 on your answer sheet.

   Q8. **What are five interesting facts you learned about America's first counties and/or Virginia's county creation process. Use complete sentences.**

Name: _____ Date: _____ Class: _____

Why Counties? – Student Answer Sheet
Directions: Use the ArcGIS Online map, "Why Counties?" to answer these questions.

Jamestown, 1607 - 1634

1. When was Jamestown founded?

2. What settlement patterns do you notice in this map? Where were people settling? Not settling?

3. What are the names of some of the settlements?

4. How far did some of the settlers live from Jamestown? How long would it take them to travel to Jamestown?

SETTLEMENT	DISTANCE	TRAVEL TIME

5. Which settlements were located farthest from Jamestown? What was their distance and travel time from Jamestown?

SETTLEMENT	DISTANCE	TRAVEL TIME

Jamestown, We Have a Problem!

6. Why did the House of Burgesses create the first counties in Virginia in 1634?

Virginia Counties, 1634 – 1890

7. *What do you notice about the location of the new counties, their shapes, and their boundaries? What are the names of the new counties? What is the root/origin of the name for these counties?*

DATE	OBSERVATIONS	INFER/WONDER
1634	Settlement Names	
1700	Settlement Names	
1750	Settlement Names	
1780	Settlement Names	

DATE	OBSERVATIONS	INFER/WONDER
1790	Settlement Names	
1860	Settlement Names	
TOPONYM		
1890	Settlement Names	

Bringing it All Together

Answer this question below on a separate sheet of paper.

8. What are five interesting facts you learned about America's first counties and/or Virginia's county creation process. Use complete sentences.

Why Counties? Answer Key

Jamestown, 1607 - 1634

1. When was Jamestown founded? **1607**
2. What settlement patterns do you notice in this map? Where were people settling? Not settling?
   Along rivers and the ocean. Primary settlement occurring along the James River
3. What are the names of some of the settlements? **Answers will vary**
4. How far did some of the settlers live from Jamestown? How long would it take them to travel to Jamestown?

SETTLEMENT	DISTANCE	TRAVEL TIME
Answers will vary	**Answers will vary**	**Answers will vary**
Answers will vary	**Answers will vary**	**Answers will vary**
Answers will vary	**Answers will vary**	**Answers will vary**

5. Which settlements were located farthest from Jamestown? What was their distance and travel time from Jamestown?

SETTLEMENT	DISTANCE	TRAVEL TIME
Answers will vary	**Answers will vary**	**Answers will vary**
Answers will vary	**Answers will vary**	**Answers will vary**
Answers will vary	**Answers will vary**	**Answers will vary**

Jamestown, We Have a Problem!

6. Why did the House of Burgesses create the first counties in Virginia in 1634?

Answers will vary. **Possible explanations include: There was only one court in Jamestown. Settlers had a long way to travel to get to court. There were too many people living in Virginia to attend one court.**

Virginia Counties, 1634 – 1890

7. *What do you notice about the location of the new counties, their shapes, and their boundaries? What are the names of the new counties? What is the root/origin of the name for these counties?*

DATE	OBSERVATIONS	INFER/WONDER
1634	Settlement: Along the James River Names: Named after England and Native Americans	Answers will vary
1700	Settlement: Settlements move north. Boundaries defined by rivers. Names: Named after England and Native Americans	Answers will vary
1750	Settlement: Growth across the Appalachian Mountains all the way to the Mississippi River. Names: England, Native Americans, and Crown Lieutenant Governors	Answers will vary
1780	Settlement: Westward to the Mississippi River and the Great Lakes. Very large counties west of the Appalachian Mountains. Names: England, Crown Officials, Virginia Governor, and Revolutionary War Heroes	Answers will vary

DATE	OBSERVATIONS	INFER/WONDER
1790	Settlement: West of Appalachian Mountains; Borders still defined by rivers. Illinois County now part of the Northwest Territory Names: French; Revolutionary War Heroes, Virginia Governors, Statesmen, and Politicians	Answers will vary
1860	Settlement: Kentucky counties are now part of Kentucky; number of counties in the Ohio River Ridge and Valley area of West Virginia. Names: US Presidents, Congressman, etc.	Answers will vary
TOPONYM	Counties near the east coast of Virginia named after England and Crown appointed officials. Further western counties named after Virginia governors, Revolutionary War heroes, France, and US elected officials. Shows the footprint of colonization, the revolutionary war, and the development of the republic	Answers will vary
1890	Settlement: West Virginia secedes; Only two counties created in Virginia. Evolution of counties complete. Names: Virginia Governor	Answers will vary

Bringing it All Together

Answer the question below on a separate sheet of paper.

8. What are five interesting facts you learned about America's first counties and/or Virginia's county creation process. Use complete sentences. **Answers will vary**

Chapter 2
Why Yorktown?

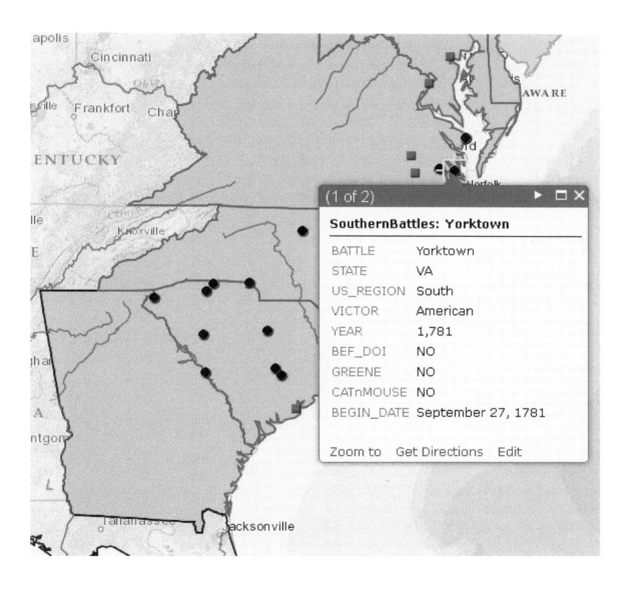

Mapping the Revolutionary War

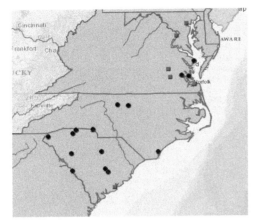

Introduction

This module provides an excellent chronological overview of the American Revolutionary War. It also focuses on how Yorktown ended up becoming the final major battle of the war. During the first lesson students filter and make observations about the battle locations for the years of 1775 – 1782. This lesson should be taught as a spring board activity or as a review of the American Revolution. We also recommend that you use this activity in conjunction with the research extension provided.

During the second lesson, "Why Yorktown," students map out and measure the distance of Nathanael Greene's movements during Britain's Southern Campaign of 1780-1781. How did Greene win the South without winning one battle? By completing this activity students will gain a better appreciation for General Greene's accomplishments and why the final battle ultimately occurred at Yorktown, Virginia.

Teacher Information

Time

- Activity One – Mapping the Revolution: 45 minutes (Use the activities in the order that makes the most sense for your classroom.)
- Activity Two – Why Yorktown: 45 minutes

Subjects
United States History

Level
Grades 5-12

Objectives
Students will be able to:

- Identify and explain the geographic distribution patterns of major American Revolutionary War battles that occurred during 1775 – 1782.
- Explain how the location of battles changed over time and provide a few explanations for the patterns of change.
- Identify and explain the geographic distribution of the battles of 1781 that occurred in the South.
- Explain how the battles of 1781 in the South contributed to General Cornwallis' decision to move his army to Yorktown, Virginia – the location of the final major battle.

Spatial Thinking Fundamentals/Themes

- Location – location of American Revolutionary War battles from 1775 – 1782.
- Region – New England, Middle, and Southern States.
- Patterns – location of American Revolutionary War battles; where are they concentrated? Where did they not occur?
- Comparison – comparing the location of battles during different phases of the American Revolutionary War.
- Distance – measuring the number of miles Cornwallis' troops traveled while chasing Nathanael Greene during 1781.

Extensions

This lesson is ripe for extending the power of ArcGIS Online. We recommend that you take advantage of ArcGIS Online's map notes functionality and assign groups of students one of the five date ranges of battles and have them identify and research specific battles, strategies, or episodes that occurred during that time period. They should then plot some of these key events into ArcGIS Online map notes and present them to their classmates. In the end you will have a great crowd-sourced map to share with parents, fellow teachers, and students.

Credits

We would like to thank Donna Shifflett, teacher for Greene County Public Schools, Virginia for researching and creating the backbone of this project while serving as "Virginia Experiment" Teaching American History Teaching Scholar. During 2007 – 2008 she researched and created the shapefiles and instructional concepts embedded in this lesson. American Revolutionary War Battles – compiled by Donna Shifflett, "The Virginia Experiment" TAH Project (Albemarle, Charlottesville, Greene, Madison, and Orange School Divisions, Virginia).

Mapping the Revolution - Instructions

Part I: Mapping the Revolution

1. Go to http://gisetc.com/mushago. Open the map, **Mapping the Revolution Part 1**. Click **Modify Map.**
2. Use the map of North America during the American Revolutionary War and the map legend to answer questions 1 and 2 on your answer sheet.

> **Q1.** **What are the general regions that the 13 original states are divided into?**
>
> **Q2.** **Which region appears to have the most cities? The least number of cities?**

Part II: The Early Battles

Let's find out where the major battles of the American Revolution were fought.

3. **Click** the **Show Contents of Map** button so that all of the layers of the map become visible.
4. Turn on ☑ the layer, **Major Battles** by checking the box to the left of the layer name.

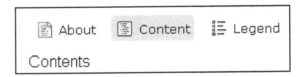

5. Look at the distribution of the major battles of the American Revolutionary War and answer question 3 on your answer sheet.

> **Q3.** **Where did the major battles of the American Revolution occur? What patterns do you notice? (Turn on and off the Major Cities layer if needed to see all of the battles.)**

The Thirteen original United States were not really states until they formall declared their independence in the Declaration of Indepence. There were some battles that occurred before the Declaration of Independence was signed on July 2, 1776.

What do you think? How many of battles on this map do you believe happened before the Declaration of Independence was signed? Provide your answer on question #4 on your worksheet.

> **Q4.** **How many Revolutionary War battles do YOU THINK occurred before the Declaration of Independence was signed?**

6. Let's find out if your selection was correct. Hover over the layer **Major Battles** and **click** on the layer. **Click** on the **Filter icon**.
7. Inside the **Filter** window create a filter that will display features in the **Major Battles layer** that match the expression **"BEF_DOI is YES"**

8. Choose **Apply Filter.**

9. Show the table of filtered results by clicking the **Show Table icon** beneath the layer name **Major Battles**.

10. Use the **map** and **table** to answer questions #5, #6, and #7. Turn on and off the Major Cities layer to help you see all of the battles that occurred.

> **Q5.** How many major battles occurred before the Declaration of Independence was signed? (HINT – SHOW THE TABLE)
>
> **Q6.** What patterns do you notice about the locations of these battles? Do you see any clusters where battles occurred? Where they did not occur?
>
> **Q7.** What were the three earliest battles of the American Revolution? Which region of the United States did they occur? (HINT – BEGIN_DATE -> SORT DESCENDING)

11. Clear the filter. To do this **click on the filter icon** below the layer **Major Battles. Select Remove Filter**.

Part III: The War for Independence, 1776 – 1780

While all of these battles were raging, King George III decided that he needed more soldiers and ships to stop the colonial rebellion. In June and July 1776, a massive British fleet arrived in New York City's harbor. This fleet consisted of 30 battleships, 1200 cannons, 30,000 soldiers, 10,000 sailors, and 300 supply ships. These troops were led by General Howe and his job was to capture New York City, cut off the colonies, and end the rebellion. Well the final battle won't occur until 1782. So General Howe and the Brits were in for a long war. Let's explore how the war played out.

After the Declaration and 1777

12. Let's look at where the battles occurred after the Declaration of Independence and into 1777.

13. Create a **filter** that matches the one in the image below:

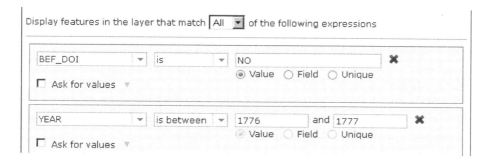

14. Choose **Apply** and use the filtered results to answer questions #8 and #9.

> **Q8.** Where did the battles occur during this time period? What patterns do you notice? Can you think of any possible explanations for the patterns you observe?
>
> **Q9.** Which colonial region and major cities are located near these battles?
>
> **Q10.** By looking at the location of these battles what do you think the strategy of the British Army was during this during this time period? What do you think they wanted to capture, protect, or control?

15. Clear the filter. To do this **click on the filter icon** below the layer **Major Battles. Select Remove Filter.**

The Battles of 1778 – 1779

16. Now let's look at where the battle theater was in 1778 - 1779. Did the general locations of battles shift or stay about the same? To do this, create a **filter** that displays features in the layer that match ALL of the following expressions:

    BEF_DOI is NO and YEAR is between 1778 and 1779.

    Use the map and table to answer questions 11, 12, and 13. Turn on and off the Major Cities layer if needed to help see all of the battles.

    Q11. Where did the battles occur during this time period? What patterns do you notice? Can you think of any possible explanations for the patterns you observe?

    Q12. Which colonial region and major cities are located near these battles?

    Q13. From looking at the location of these battles what do you think the strategies of the British or American Armies were during this part of the war? What did they want to capture, protect, or control?

17. Clear the filter. To do this **click on the filter icon** below the layer **Major Battles. Select Remove Filter.**

The Battles of 1780

18. Let's look at where the battle theater was in 1780. Did the general locations of battles shift or stay about the same as 1778 - 1779? To do this, create a **filter** that displays features in the layer that match ALL of the following expressions:

    BEF_DOI is NO and YEAR is 1780.

    Use the map and table to answer questions 14, 15, and 16. Turn on and off the Major Cities layer if needed to help see all of the battles.

    Q14. Where did the battles occur during this time period? What patterns do you notice? Can you think of any possible explanations for the patterns you observe?

    Q15. Which colonial region and major cities are located near these battles?

    Q16. From looking at the location of these battles what do you think the strategies of the British or American Armies were during this part of the war? What did they want to capture, protect, or control?

19. Clear the filter. To do this **click on the filter icon** below the layer **Major Battles. Select Remove Filter.**

The Battles of 1781 and 1782

20. Let's look at where the war's final battles will occur. To do this, create a **filter** that displays features in the layer that match ALL of the following expressions:

    BEF_DOI is NO and YEAR is between 1781 and 1782.

21. Use the map and table to answer questions 17, 18, and 19. Turn on ☑ and off ☐ the **Major Cities** layer if needed to help see all of the battles.

    Q17. Where did the battles occur during this time period? What patterns do you notice? Can you think of any possible explanations for the patterns you observe?
    Q18. Which colonial region and major cities are located near these battles?
    Q19. From looking at the location of these battles what do you think the strategies of the British or American Armies were during this part of the war? What did they want to capture, protect, or control?
    Q20. When and where did the final three battles of the American Revolution occur?

22. Clear the filter. To do this **click on the filter icon** below the layer **Major Battles. Select Remove Filter**.

Bringing it All Together

Using the answers from this activity and the maps you looked at write a short paragraph that describes how the locations of the battles and strategies of the American Revolution changed from 1775 - 1782.

Name: _____ Date: _____ Class: _____

Mapping the Revolution – Student Answer Sheet

Directions: Use the ArcGIS Online map titled Why Yorktown: Mapping the American Revolution to answer the following questions.

The United States in 1776

Q1. What are the general regions that the 13 original states are divided into?

Q2. Which region appears to have the most cities? Which one has the least number of cities?

Before the Declaration of Independence

Q3. Where did the major battles of the American Revolution occur? What patterns do you notice?

Q4. How many Revolutionary War battles on this map do you THINK occurred before the Declaration of Independence was signed on July 2, 1776? Circle one of the following:

      1   9   17   28   52

Q5. How many major battles occurred before the Declaration of Independence was signed?

Q6. What patterns do you notice about where the battles occurred? Do you see any clusters where battles occurred? Where they did not occur?

Q7. What were the three earliest battles of the American Revolution? Which region of the United States did they occur?

After the Declaration and 1777

Q8. Where did the battles occur during this time period? What patterns do you notice? Can you think of any possible explanations for the patterns you observe?

Q9. Which colonial region and major cities are located near these battles?

Q10. By looking at this map what do you think the strategies of the American and British Armies were during this portion of the war? What did either side want to capture, protect, or control?

1778 – 1779

Q11. Where did the battles occur during this time period? What patterns do you notice? Can you think of any possible explanations for the patterns you observe?

Q12. Which colonial region and major cities are located near these battles?

Q13. By looking at this map what do you think the strategies of the American and British Armies were during this portion of the war? What did they want to capture, protect, or control?

1780

Q14. Where did the battles occur during this time period? What patterns do you notice? Can you think of any possible explanations for the patterns you observe?

Q15. Which colonial region and major cities are located near these battles?

Q16. By looking at this map what do you think the strategies of the American and British Armies were during this portion of the war? What did either side want to capture, protect, or control?

1781 – 1782

Q17. Where did the battles occur during this time period? What patterns do you notice? Can you think of any possible explanations for the patterns you observe?

Q18. Which colonial region and major cities are located near these battles?

Q19. By looking at this map what do you think the strategies of the American and British Armies were during this portion of the war? What did either side want to capture, protect, or control?

Q20. When and where did the final three battles of the American Revolution occur?

Bringing it All Together

Using the answers from this activity and the maps to write a short paragraph that describes how the locations of the battles and strategies of the American Revolution changed from 1775 - 1782.

Mapping the Revolution Answer Key

The United States in 1776

Q1. What are the general regions that the 13 original states are divided into? **New England, Middle, and Southern**

Q2. Which region appears to have the most cities? The least number of cities? **Most: New England and Middle; Least: Southern**

Before the Declaration of Independence

Q3. Where did the major battles of the American Revolution occur? What patterns do you notice? **Answers will vary. Possible patterns include: Mostly occur in the 13 original colonies; Cluster of battles in between New York City and Philadelphia; cluster of battles along the Hudson River, NY; other clusters appear to occur along rivers, cities, and the coast; Not many battles in Virginia, Maryland, or Delaware.**

Q4. How many Revolutionary War battles on this map do you THINK occurred before the Declaration of Independence was signed on July 2, 1776? Circle one of the following: **Answers will vary.**

Q5. How many major battles occurred before the Declaration of Independence was signed? **17**

Q6. What patterns do you notice about where the battles occurred? Do you see any clusters where battles occurred? Where they did not occur? **Answers will vary. Possible patterns include: The majority of these battles occur in New England; a concentration of battles around Boston; a few battles located in the Middle and Southern colonies.**

Q7. What were the three earliest battles of the American Revolution? Which region of the United States did they occur? **Lexington/Concord, Boston, Fort Ticonderoga; New England (and border of Middle Colonies).**

After the Declaration and 1777

Q8. Where did the battles occur during this time period? What patterns do you notice? Can you think of any possible explanations for the patterns you observe? **Answers will vary. Possible patterns and explanations include: Most of battles occur between Lake Champlain and Philadelphia; battles are occurring along waterways and around the big cities of New York and Philadelphia. American strategy is to protect the important cities. British strategy is to capture New York and Philadelphia.**

Q9. Which colonial region and major cities are located near these battles? **Middle Colonies; New York City and Philadelphia**

Q10. By looking at this map what do you think the strategies of the American and British Armies were during this portion of the war? What did either side want to capture, protect, or control? **Answers will vary. Possible ideas include: American strategy is to protect the important cities. British strategy is to capture New York and Philadelphia while also controlling waterways.**

1778 – 1779

Q11. Where did the battles occur during this time period? What patterns do you notice? Can you think of any possible explanations for the patterns you observe? **Answers will vary. Possible patterns include: Battles are still occurring mostly along the rivers and waterways around and between New York City and Philadelphia; A few battles are occurring out on the frontier. The farthest western battle was Kaskaskia.**

Q12. Which colonial region and major cities are located near these battles? **Middle; Philadelphia and New York City**

Q13. By looking at this map what do you think the strategies of the American and British Armies were during this portion of the war? What did they want to capture, protect, or control? **Answers will vary. Possible ideas include: American strategy is to protect the important cities. British strategy is to capture New York and Philadelphia while also controlling waterways. Also appears that the Americans and British have an interest in controlling the forts and posts near the Great Lakes and Ohio River**

1780

Q14. Where did the battles occur during this time period? What patterns do you notice? Can you think of any possible explanations for the patterns you observe? **Answers will vary. Possible observations include: Less fighting occurring in New England and Middle Colonies; High concentration of battles in South Carolina. One battle in Mobile Alabama (note that the SPANISH won this battle!)**

Q15. Which colonial region and major cities are located near these battles? **Southern; less fighting around cities. A couple of battles outside of Philadelphia.**

Q16. By looking at this map what do you think the strategies of the American and British Armies were during this portion of the war? What did either side want to capture, protect, or control? **Looks like the American army wants to protect the South. The British want to capture the South.**

1781 – 1782

Q17. Where did the battles occur during this time period? What patterns do you notice? Can you think of any possible explanations for the patterns you observe? **Answers will vary. Possible observations include: Less fighting occurring in New England and Middle Colonies; High concentration of battles in South Carolina. One battle occurred along the Gulf Coast (note that the SPANISH won this battle!); a cluster of battles occur near the Chesapeake Bay and in Virginia.**

Q18. Which colonial region and major cities are located near these battles? **Southern Colonies; possible cities of importance include Norfolk, VA and possibly Charleston, SC**

Q19. By looking at this map what do you think the strategies of the American and British Armies were during this portion of the war? What did either side want to capture, protect, or control? **Americans wanted to protect South Carolina and the Chesapeake Bay. The British wanted to capture/control the Southern Colonies and port cities.**

Q20 When and where did the final four battles of the American Revolution occur? **Virginia, New York, and South Carolina. They occurred between September, 1781 and October, 1782.**

Bringing it All Together

Using the answers from this activity and the maps you looked at write a short paragraph that describes how the locations of the battles and strategies of the American Revolution changed between 1775 - 1782. **Answers will vary. Possible answers should include: the first phase of the war occurred in New England; the second phase occurred in the Middle states; the final phase occurred in the South with sporadic fighting in the Middle and New England states.**

Why Yorktown? – Instructions
Background Reading

Courtesy of Donna Shifflett, Greene County Public Schools, Virginia

Much attention is given to the surrender of General Lord Charles Cornwallis to General George Washington, but there is no mention of how and why the location of Yorktown was chosen. In actuality, he was forced to retreat northward after chasing General Nathanael Greene's army throughout the Southern states.

General Nathanael Greene became the Commander of the South on December 2, 1780 and set out to lure Cornwallis away from his supplies. Greene (mouse) began a "cat and mouse" chase with Lord Cornwallis (cat), who had supply depots in Charleston, South Carolina and Wilmington, North Carolina. He also had almost complete control of the state of North Carolina. Greene's plan was to keep Cornwallis away from his source of supplies. He split his army in two, placing General Daniel Morgan in charge of one-half. His plan was to have Cornwallis follow him, taking General Cornwallis further and further away from his supply stations.

In January 1781, he sent Morgan's men to Cowpens, SC, where they defeated a British army in the Battle of Cowpens on January 17. From there Cornwallis and his troops followed the Colonial troops across the Southern countryside getting further and further from their supplies in enemy territory. For approximately two months Greene's troops used this strategy against Redcoats. At one point Cornwallis' troops actually burned their provisions in order to travel more quickly so they could keep up with Greene's whereabouts.

During the next 30 minutes or so you will explore General Greene's strategy, but first **answer questions 1 – 3** on the student answer sheet.

Q1. Who was in charge of British troops during the Southern Campaign? Who was in command of the American troops?

Q2. Why were the cities of Charleston, South Carolina and Wilmington, North Carolina important to the British?

Q3. Why did the American general split his army in half?

The Race to the Dan
1. Go to http://gisetc.com/mushago. Open the map, **Why Yorktown.** Click **Modify Map.**

2. Click the **Show Contents of Map** button so that all of the layers of the map become visible.

3. The map you are looking at shows the major battles that occurred during Britain's **Southern Campaign.** To explore Nathanael Greene's "Cat and Mouse" strategy you need to filter the layer, "Southern Campaign," to only show the "Cat and Mouse" battles.

4. Hover over the layer **Southern Campaign** and **click** on the layer to bring up the options and **click** the **Filter icon.**

5. Inside the **Filter** window create a filter that will display features in the Southern Campaign layer that match the expression **"CATnMOUSE is YES"**

6. Choose **Apply Filter.**

7. Show the table of filtered results by clicking the **Show Table icon** below the layer **Southern Campaign**. Use this table to **answer questions 4-5.**

   Q4. **How many major battles were involved in this strategy?**
   Q5. **In which states did these battles occur?**

8. Next you are going to map out the chase that Nathanael Greene took the British troops on. To do this you will need to complete these three steps for each leg of Greene's strategy.

   - One by one, turn on ☑ each key stage/leg of the chase.
   - Add (draw) lines on the map showing where Greene's troops and Cornwallis' troops traveled.
   - Use the measure tool to calculate the distance Greene's troops traveled and fill in the chart.

9. The British chase of Greene began following the Battle of Cowpens. Turn on ☑ the layer Cowpens. From there they followed Greene's troops to Cowan's Ford. Turn on ☑ Cowan's Ford. Now you're ready to draw and measure the first leg.

10. **To draw a line on the map you need to add a map notes layer.** To do this, choose **Add** then **Add Map Notes.** Add a Map Note layer and name it **The Chase**.

11. Choose **Create**
12. Name the line **"Cowpens to Cowan's Ford"**
13. **Close** the **Add Feature Window** and return to the Content
14. (Layers) of the map.
15. Use the measure tool to calculate the distance that Greene's troops traveled during this leg. **Complete row A in question 6.**

In an effort to buy time and to allow his army to gain strength from other militias in the South, Greene set out to towards the Dan River at the North Carolina/Virginia border. His goals were to get to the northern side of the river before Cornwallis could, while also getting the British army further and further from their supplies.

Let's map this leg of the chase.

16. Turn on the layer, Crossing the Dan.
17. Click on the "Cowpens to Cowan's Ford" line that you just drew and choose **Edit**. Choose to **add** a new **free hand line** and draw a line from **Cowan's Ford** point to the **Crossing the Dan** point. Name this line **"Race to the Dan River." Close** the **Add Feature** window.
18. Use the measure tool to calculate the distance that Greene's troops traveled during this leg. **Complete row B in question 6.**

Greene will spend about a week resting his troops at Halifax Courthouse, Virginia. After some rest his troops will set out to push Cornwallis north towards Guilford Courthouse in North Carolina. Along the way they get into a small battle with British troops at Haw's River, NC. Let's map out this leg of the chase.

19. Turn on the layers Haw's River and Guilford Courthouse.
20. Click on the any of the lines you've already drawn and choose **Edit**. Choose to **add** a new **free hand line** and draw a line from **Crossing the Dan** point to **Haw's River** and **Guilford Courthouse**. Name this line **"To Guilford Courthouse."** **Close** the **Add Feature** window

21. Use the measure tool to calculate the distance that Greene's troops traveled during this leg. **Complete row C in question 6.**

Cornwallis and the Redcoats will win the Battle at Guilford Courthouse. This victory came with a high price tag – the British lost about 25% of their men. Following this battle Cornwallis will decide he must get his troops closer to their supplies. Following this battle his troops will set out for Wilmington, NC. Let's map his retreat to Wilmington on the map.

22. **Turn on** the layer **Wilmington, NC.**
23. Click on the **any of the lines** you've already drawn and choose **Edit**. Choose to **add** a new **free hand line** and draw a line from **Guilford Courthouse** to **Wilmington, NC.** Name this line **"Cornwallis returns to Wilmington."** Make this line a thicker red line to represent the Redcoats. **Close** the **Add Feature** window

Greene considered following Cornwallis to Wilmington, but decides instead to head south to fight the other British troops stationed throughout the Carolinas. Let's map out where Greene's troops will head to after Guilford Courthouse. Let's map the last few legs of Greene's Southern Campaign.

24. **Turn on** the layer **Hobkirk's Hill.**
25. Click on the **any of the lines** you've already drawn and choose **Edit**. Choose to **add** a new **free hand line** and draw a line from **Guilford Courthouse** to **Augusta** and **Hobkirk's Hill.** Name this line **"to Hobkirk's Hill"** **Close** the **Add Feature** window

26. Use the **measure tool** to calculate the distance that Greene's troops traveled during this leg. **Complete row D in question 6.** Also record which side won the battle.

The day after Hobkirk's Hill, Cornwallis (he didn't know about the result) will decide to leave the Carolinas and try to regroup with British troops near the Chesapeake. He will select Yorktown, Virginia as his destination. Let's draw a line connecting Wilmington to Yorktown showing Cornwallis' movement.

27. Filter the Southern Campaign Battles layer to display features in the layer that match the following expression: **"BATTLE is Yorktown."**

28. Draw a line that connects **Wilmington, NC** to **Yorktown, VA.** Name this line "**Cornwallis Moves to Yorktown.**" Make this line a **thicker red line** to represent the Redcoats. **Close** the **Add Feature** window.

After Hobkirk's Hill, Greene will try to retake the South Carolina outpost town of Ninety-Six.
29. Draw a line from **Hobkirk's Hill** to **Ninety-Six.** Name this line **"to Ninety-Six." Close** the **Add Feature** window.

30. Use the **measure tool** to **calculate** how many miles Greene's men marched to get to **Ninety-Six. Complete Row E in question 6.** Also record which side won the battle.

The last battle that Greene will be engaged in will be Eutaw Springs.   In fact it will be the last major battle south of Virginia.

31. Turn on the layer **Eutaw Springs.**
32. Click on the **any of the lines** you've already drawn and choose **Edit**. Choose to **add** a new **free hand line** and draw a line from **Ninety-Six** to **Eutaw Springs**. Name this line **"to Eutaw Springs"** **Close** the **Add Feature** window.

33. Use the **measure** tool to **calculate** the distance that Greene's troops traveled during this leg. **Complete row F in question 6.** Also record which side won the battle.

Nice job! You have just created a map that shows the key locations that Nathanael Greene's troops marched towards. Now use this map to help answer the two primary focus questions.

34. Turn on ☑ the layer "Primary Sources." Notice two primary source placemarks become visible.
35. Click on the primary source next to **Yorktown, Virginia**. Use this image to **answer question 7** on your worksheet.

> **Q7.** **What conclusions can you draw from this image about Cornwallis' experience at Yorktown?**

36. Next, click on the primary source placemark located near the coast of South Carolina. Use this quote and the paths you drew to **answer questions 8 and 9.**

> **Q8.** **How does the map you drew support Greene's quote about his strategy in the South?**

> **Q9.** **Why Yorktown? How did Nathanael Greene's strategy in the South help the American Patriots defeat General Cornwallis at Yorktown and ultimately win the American Revolution? Identify at least two examples from the map and explain their importance.**

Name: _____ Date: _____ Class: _____

Why Yorktown? Student Answer Sheet
Directions: Use the ArcGIS Online map titled Why Yorktown: Mapping the American Revolution to answer the following questions.

Background Reading

1. Who was in charge of British troops during the Southern Campaign? Who was in command of the American troops?

2. Why were the cities of Charleston, South Carolina and Wilmington, North Carolina important to the British?

3. Why did the American general split his army in half?

The Southern Campaign

4. How many major battles were involved in this strategy?

5. In which states did these battles occur?

6. As you draw each leg of Greene's strategy complete this chart.

ROW	MILES TRAVELED	KEY BATTLE	VICTOR
A			
B			
C			
D			
E			
F			

7. What conclusions can you draw from this image about Cornwallis' experience at Yorktown?

8. How does your map support this quote from Nathanael Greene?

9. Why Yorktown? How did Nathanael Greene's strategy in the South help the American Patriots defeat General Cornwallis at Yorktown and ultimately win the American Revolution? **Identify at least two examples from the map and explain their importance.**

Why Yorktown? Answer Key

Background Reading

1. Who was in charge of British troops during the Southern Campaign? Who was in command of the American troops? **British – Charles Cornwallis; American – Nathanael Greene**
2. Why were the cities of Charleston, South Carolina and Wilmington, North Carolina important to the British? **They were cities along the coast where the army had plenty of supplies and support.**
3. Why did the American general split his army in half? **The take the British further away from the coast and their supplies.**

The Southern Campaign

4. How many major battles were involved in this strategy? **8**
5. In which states did these battles occur? **The Southern States (South Carolina, Georgia, North Carolina, and Virginia.**

6. As you draw each leg of Greene's strategy complete this chart.

ROW	MILES TRAVELED	KEY BATTLE	VICTOR
A	~50 Miles	Cowan's Ford	British
B	~159 Miles	None	None
C	~78 Miles	Guilford Courthouse	British
D	~143 Miles	Hobkirk's Hill	British
E	~161 Miles	Ninety Six	British
F	~110 Miles	Eutaw Springs	British

7. What conclusions can you draw from this image about Cornwallis' experience at Yorktown? **Cornwallis had to surrender his Army at Yorktown**
8. How does your map support this quote from Nathanael Greene? **Answers will vary. Possible explanations include: Greene's troops traveled over 700 miles leading the British from North Carolina to Virginia back to North Carolina and then into South Carolina.**
9. Why Yorktown? How did Nathanael Greene's strategy in the South help the American Patriots defeat General Cornwallis at Yorktown and ultimately win the American Revolution? **Identify at least two examples from the map and explain their importance. Answers will vary. Possible examples include: Cornwallis's troops became tired and under-supplied chasing Greene across the Southern countryside; Cornwallis's troops marched over 500 miles and didn't have much to show for it; They chose Yorktown as a place to regroup only to meet their final defeat.**

Chapter 3
Mapping the Constitutional Convention

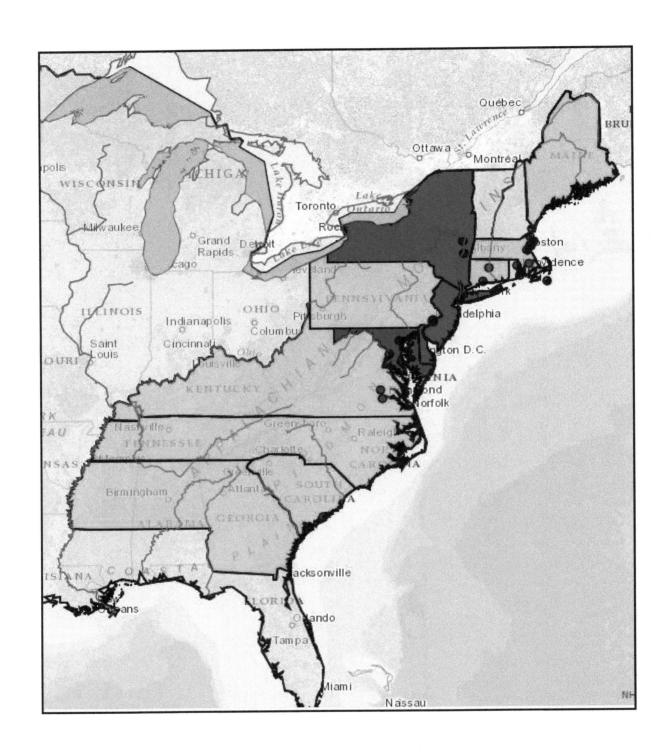

Mapping the Constitutional Convention

Introduction
The students will understand the basic principles and compromises that went into the creation of the Constitution of the United States. A complete understanding of the ideas and compromises will allow students to better appreciate the issues that caused sectionalism during westward expansion and eventually led to secession and the Civil War.

Teacher Information

Time
- Activity One: United States, 1787
- Activity Two: New Jersey Plan vs. Virginia Plan
- Activity Three: Great Compromise
- Activity Four: 3/5 Compromise

Subjects
United States History, United States Government

Level
Grades 5-12

Objectives
Students will be able to:
- Explain the basic principles and compromises that went into the creation of the Constitution of the United States.
- Identify and explain the differing perspectives found at the Constitutional Convention: large states vs. small states, free states vs. slave states

Spatial Thinking Fundamentals/Themes
- Location – location of big cities and port cities, states with the highest population, states with the lowest population
- Region – areas of free states; areas of slave states;
- Patterns – Constitutional Convention votes
- Comparison – votes made by large states and small states, free states and slave states

Mapping the Constitutional Convention: United States, 1787 - Instructions

Part I: Population Distribution

1. Go to http://gisetc.com/mushago. Open the map, **Mapping the Constitutional Convention**. Click **Modify Map**.
2. In front of you is a map of the original 13 states. Use the map and the information located in the tables to answer questions 1- 12.
3. **Click** the **Show Contents of Map** button so that all of the layers of the map become visible.
4. Hover over and click on the **United States, 1790 layer**. **Click** on the **Show Table icon**.
5. Use this table to answer questions 1 – 4.

> **Q1.** Which state has the highest population? What is the population of that state? (HINT– sort TOT_POP to sort descending)
>
> **Q2.** Which state has the smallest population? What is the population of that state? (HINT – sort TOT_POP to sort ascending)
>
> **Q3.** List the states that have the 4 highest and 4 lowest population totals.
>
> **Q4.** What states had fewer than 200,000 people?

6. Close the table.
7. Use the **Large Cities 1790** layer and the base map to help you answer questions 5-6.

> **Q5.** What patterns do you notice regarding major cities in 1790? What are some explanations for those patterns?
>
> **Q6.** What states had cities with more than 10,000 people? What is similar about their location?

Part II: Slavery

8. Hover over and click on the layer **United States 1790**. Click on the **Show Table icon**.
9. Use the table on the answer sheet to complete questions 8-12.

> **Q7.** Which state has the highest slave population? How many slaves are in that state? (HINT – sort SLAVES to sort descending)
>
> **Q8.** Which states has the smallest slave population? How many slaves are in that state? (HINT – sort SLAVES to sort ascending)
>
> **Q9.** List the states that have the four highest and four lowest slave totals.
>
> **Q10.** Where are there more slaves? Why?
>
> **Q11.** In which states do slaves make up 25% or more of the population? (HINT – sort SLV_PCT to sort descending)
>
> **Q12.** Which states have more than 200,000 people and fewer than 100,000 slaves?

Part III: So What?

Looking over the information you've compiled, why do you think it might matter when it comes to revising the Articles of Confederation or writing a new constitution?

Q13.   How do you think the needs and wants of large states and small states might be different? How might they be similar?

Q14.   How do you think the needs and wants of states with large numbers of slaves might be different than those states with a small (or no) number of slaves? How might they be similar?

The Constitutional Convention: New Jersey Plan vs. Virginia Plan – Instructions

Part I: May 30-Should a national government be established consisting of a supreme legislative, executive, and judiciary?

A convention was called for the purpose of revising and amending the Articles of Confederation. By the end of May, 1787 eight states had sent delegates. Delegates from New Hampshire, Maryland, New Jersey and Georgia had not yet arrived. Rhode Island chose not to participate in this convention.

On the first day of voting, delegates voted on the question of what the new government would look like. The Articles of Confederation had neither an executive nor a judicial branch. States that voted 'yes' here would be voting for a complete overhaul, if not complete overthrow of the Articles of Confederation.

States sent more than one person to the convention. The delegates did not always agree on their vote. This would lead to a divided vote (DIV) by the state.

1. **Go to** http://gisetc.com/mushago. Open the map, **Mapping the Constitutional Convention**. Click **Modify Map**.
2. Click the **Show Contents of Map** button so that all of the layers of the map become visible.
3. Use the map of the original 13 states to help you make predictions on how a sampling of states will vote on the question *"Should a national government be established consisting of a supreme legislative, executive, and judiciary?"*
4. Based on what you know about the Articles of Confederation and the demographics of the states involved, how do you think states will vote on this question? Be prepared to defend your predictions based on data.

    Q1. **Make your predictions about state votes on the chart.**

5. Hover over and click on the layer named **United States, 1790**. Click on the **Change Style icon**.
6. For **Choose an attribute to show** click on the drop down arrow and **select the variable "SLEG"**
7. For **Select a Drawing Style** click on **Options** under **Types (Unique Values)**
8. **Click Done Changing Symbols.**
9. Click on the **layer name** and click on the **Show Legend icon**.
10. Use the map to add additional information to your chart and to answer additional questions.

    Q2. **Update the chart to reflect how states actually voted.**
    Q3. **What pattern do you see to this vote? What might explain the way states voted?**

Part II: June 19 - Should states revise and amend the Articles of Confederation? Should we use the New Jersey Plan?

The states have been debating for almost a month now. The first vote they took essentially gutted the Articles of Confederation. Three weeks later, another vote was taken as to whether or not they should revise and amend the Articles of Confederation. This vote would be seen as endorsement of the New Jersey Plan.

The **Virginia Plan** calls for three branches of government: legislative, executive, and judicial.	The **New Jersey Plan** calls for three branches of government: legislative, executive, and judicial.
• There should be two houses (bicameral) in the legislative branch. Representation in both houses will be based on population. • Calls for a single executive (President). • The executive can be removed by impeachment and conviction. • Will be ratified by the people themselves. This plan would constitute a complete replacement of the Articles of Confederation.	• The legislative branch will consist of one house (unicameral) and all states will be represented equally. • Calls for an executive branch that will consist of more than one person (the exact number is up for debate) • Will be ratified by the states. This plan was seen by many as a way of simply revising the Articles of Confederation rather than

11. After reading the short explanations in the boxes, answer the following questions.

Q4. Which states does the Virginia Plan favor?
Q5. Which states does the New Jersey Plan favor?

12. Based on what you know about the Articles of Confederation and the demographics of the states involved, make predictions on how a sampling of states will vote on the question - Should states revise and amend the Articles of Confederation?

Q6. Make your predictions about state votes on the chart.

13. Hover over and click on the layer named **United States 1790**. Click on **Change Style icon.**
14. For **Choose an attribute to show** click on the drop down arrow and **select the variable "AoCRev."**
15. For **Select a Drawing Style** click on **Options** under **Types (Unique Values)**
16. **Click Done Changing Symbols.**
17. Click on the **layer name** and click on the **Show Legend icon.**
18. Use the map to add additional information to your chart and to answer additional questions.

Q7. Update the chart to reflect how states actually voted.
Q8. What pattern do you see to this vote? What might explain the way states voted?
Q9. Why might states with large populations have voted for the New Jersey Plan?

Part III: June 19 - Should states use the Virginia Plan without alteration? Should we ignore the New Jersey Plan?

After the last vote, a motion is made to use the Virginia Plan without changing it, essentially asking the delegates to ignore the New Jersey Plan.

19. Hover over and click on the layer named **United States 1790.** Click on the **Change Style icon.**
20. For **Choose an attribute to show** click on the drop down arrow and **select the variable "NJVA"**
21. For **Select a Drawing Style** click on **Options** under **Types (Unique Values)**
22. **Click Done Changing Symbols.**
23. Click on the **layer name** and click on the **Show Legend icon.**
24. Use the map to answer the following questions.

   Q10. **What patterns do you see in the voting?**
   Q11. **Why might states with large populations have voted for the Virginia Plan?**

Extension Activities

Optional discussion questions:

1. What are the benefits of the Virginia Plan?
2. Who benefits from the Virginia Plan?
3. What are the benefits of the New Jersey Plan?
4. Who benefits from the New Jersey Plan
5. Are there more small states or large states?
6. Can the small states band together and force the New Jersey Plan on the large states?
7. Can the larger states band together and force the Virginia Plan on the small states?
8. What compromises can be negotiated that would make both small and large states happy?

The Constitutional Convention: The Great Compromise – Instructions

Part I: June 11- Should all states have one vote in the Senate, regardless of size?
Some decisions about the legislative branch have been made. In one house of the legislative branch, states will be represented based on population. It is not as simple as counting the people who live in each state. States must now decide how or if they will count the slaves in each state.

1. Go to http://gisetc.com/mushago. Open the map, **Mapping the Constitutional Convention**. Click **Modify Map**.
2. In front of you is a map of the original 13 states. Use the map and information from the tables to answer the following questions.

Let's do a quick review of the state populations.

3. **Click** the **Show the Contents of Map** button so that all of the layers of the map become visible.
4. Hover over and click on the layer named **United States 1790**. Click on the **Show Table icon**.
5. **Click** on TOT_POP and sort ascending to get a quick look at the population of each state.
6. Based on population, predict which states will vote "no" and which states will vote "yes" on the question, *"Should all states have one vote in the Senate, regardless of size?"*
   Q1.   Make your predictions about state votes on the chart.

7. Hover over and click on the layer named **United States, 1790**. Click on the **Change Style icon**.
8. For **Choose an attribute to show** click on the drop down arrow and **select the variable "S1Vote"**
9. For **Select a Drawing Style** click on **Options** under **Types (Unique Values)**
10. **Click Done Changing Symbols.**
11. Click on the **layer name** and click on the **Show Legend icon**.
12. Use the map to add additional information to your chart and to answer additional questions.

   Q2.   Update the chart to reflect how the states actually voted.
   Q3.   What patterns do you see in how states voted? What might explain these votes?
   Q4.   Can you think of a reason why South Carolina might have voted no? Does it make sense that a small state would vote not to have equal representation in the Senate?

Part II: June 11- Should states have representation based on population in the Senate?

13. Delaware has 59,096 people. Virginia has 821,227. Let's say that for every 50,000 people in your state you will get one representative in the Senate. Use this information to answer the following questions

   Q5.   How many delegates would Delaware get?
   Q6.   How many delegates would Virginia get?

14. Based on the results of the last vote, predict which states will vote "no" and which states will vote "yes" on the question, *"Should states have representation based on population in the Senate?"*
   Q7.   Make your predictions about state votes on the chart.

15. Hover over and **click** on the layer named **United States, 1790**. **Click** on the **Change Style icon**.

16. For **Choose an attribute to show** click on the drop down arrow and **select the variable "PRPREP"**
17. For **Select a Drawing Style** click on **Options** under **Types (Unique Values)**
18. **Click Done Changing Symbols.**
19. Click on the **layer name** and click on the **Show Legend icon.**
20. Use the map to add additional information to your chart and to answer additional questions.

Q8.   Update the chart to reflect how the states actually voted.

Q9.   What patterns do you see in how states voted? What might explain these votes?

Q10. Can you think of a reason why Connecticut might have voted for proportional representation? Does it make sense that a small state would vote for representation based on population?

Q11. Who benefits from states being equally represented in the Senate? Who does not benefit?

Q12. Do you think it's fair for very small numbers of people to make decisions for large numbers of people?

Q13. Do you think it's fair for people who live in small states to have very little decision-making power when compared to large states?

Q14. How can you make the legislative branch work for all states – no matter what size they are?

The Constitutional Convention: The 3/5 Compromise – Instructions

States are debating how they will be represented in Congress. The small states prefer that all states have equal representation in Congress. Larger states prefer that representation be decided based on population. How will they solve this problem?

Note: The New York delegates left the convention on July 3 and did not return.

Part I: July 10 - Should whites equal slaves for the apportionment of representation?

1. Go to http://gisetc.com/mushago. Open the map, **Mapping the Constitutional Convention**. Click **Modify Map.**

Let's do a quick review of how many slaves were found in each state and what percentage they were of the total population.

Use map of the original 13 states and information from the tables to answer the following questions.

2. **Click** the **Show Contents of Map** button so that all of the layers of the map become visible.
3. Hover over and **click** on the layer named **United States, 1790. Click** on the **Show Table icon.**
4. **Click** on **SLAVES** and sort descending to get a quick look at the population of each state. Skim the list to look for states with large numbers of slaves.
5. **Click** on **SLV_PCT** and sort descending to get a quick look at what percentage slaves were of the total population.
6. Based on the number of slaves and their percentage of the total population, predict which states will vote "no" and which states will vote "yes" on the question, *"Should whites equal slaves for the apportionment of representation?"*
    Q1.   Make your predictions about state votes on the chart.

8. Hover over and **click** on the layer named **United States, 1790. Click** on the **Change Style icon.**
9. For **Choose an attribute to show** click on the drop down arrow and **select the variable "AAEQWHT"**
10. For **Select a Drawing Style** click on **Options** under **Types (Unique Values)**
11. **Click Done Changing Symbols.**
12. Click on the **layer name** and click on the **Show Legend icon.**
13. Use the map to add additional information to your chart and to answer additional questions.
    Q2.   Update the chart to reflect how the states actually voted.
    Q3.   What patterns do you see in how states voted? What might explain these votes?
    Q4.   Can you think of a reason why Virginia and North Carolina might have voted the way they did?

Part II: July 10 - Should slaves count as 3/5 of a person for the apportionment of representation?

7. **Click** the **Show Content of Map** button so that all of the layers of the map become visible.
8. Hover over and **click** on the layer named **United States, 1790. Click** on the **Show Table icon.**
9. Based on the number of slaves, their percentage of the total population and the outcome of the last vote, predict which states will vote "no" and which states will vote "yes" on the question, *"Should slaves count as 3/5 of a person for the apportionment of representation?"*
   Q5. **Make your predictions about state votes on the chart.**

14. Hover over and **click** on the layer named **United States, 1790. Click** on the **Change Style icon.**
15. For **Choose an attribute to show** click on the drop down arrow and **select the variable "AA35"**
16. For **Select a Drawing Style** click on **Options** under **Types (Unique Values)**
17. **Click Done Changing Symbols.**
18. Click on the **layer name** and click on the **Show Legend icon.**
19. Use the map to add additional information to your chart and to answer additional questions.

   Q6. **Update the chart to reflect how the states actually voted.**
   Q7. **What patterns do you see in how states voted? What might explain these votes?**
   Q8. **Why might be driving Southern states to vote yes for this proposal?**
   Q9. **Why do you think South Carolina is the only state to vote no? What is different about South Carolina than other slave-holding states?**

Extension
Answer these questions as if you were a delegate at the Constitutional Convention from the
State of _____.

1. Do you count slaves?
2. Should you count slaves as part of a state's population? Why or why not?
3. What if the number of slaves would greatly increase the amount of representation your state would have in the legislature?
4. What if the number of slaves would greatly increase the amount of representation another state would have in the legislature?
5. What if you had to pay a tax on the slaves in your state?
6. What if you could charge people in other states a tax on slaves?

Name: _____ Date: _____ Class: _____

Constitutional Convention: United States, 1787 – Student Answer Sheet

Directions: Use the ArcGIS Online map titled The Constitutional Convention to answer the following questions.

1. Which state has the highest total population? What is the population of that state?

State	Number of people

2. Which state has the smallest population? What is the population of that state?

State	Number of people

3. List the states that have the 4 highest and 4 lowest population totals.

States w/highest population	States w/lowest population

4. What states had fewer than 200,000 people?

States	How are they similar?	How are they different?

5. What patterns do you notice regarding major cities in 1790? What are some explanations for those patterns?

Patterns	Explanations

6. What states had cities with more than 10,000 people? What is similar about their location?

7. Which state has the highest slave population? How many slaves are in that state?

State	Number of slaves

8. Which state has the smallest slave population? How many slaves are in that state?

State	Number of slaves

9. List the states that have the 4 highest and 4 lowest slave totals.

States w/highest slave population	States w/lowest slave population

10. Where are there more slaves? Why?

11. In which states do slaves make up 25% or more of the population?

12. Which states have more than 200,000 people and fewer than 100,000 slaves?

13. How do you think the needs and wants of large states and small states might be similar? How might they be different?

Similarities	Differences

14. How do you think the needs and wants of states with large numbers of slaves might be similar than states with a small number (or no) of slaves? How might they be different?

Similarities	Differences

Name: _____ Date: _____ Class: _____

Constitutional Convention: New Jersey Plan vs. Virginia Plan – Student Answer Sheet

Directions: Use the ArcGIS Online map titled, "The Constitutional Convention," to answer the following questions.

1. Make your predictions about state votes on the chart.
2. After you've updated your ArcGIS map, update the chart to reflect how states actually voted.

May 30: Should a national government be established consisting of a supreme legislative, executive, and judiciary?						
State	Yes		No		Divided	
	Prediction	Actual	Prediction	Actual	Prediction	Actual
Massachusetts						
Connecticut						
New York						
Delaware						
Pennsylvania						
Virginia						
North Carolina						
South Carolina						

3. What pattern do you see to this vote? What might explain the way states voted?

Patterns	Explanation

4. Which states does the Virginia Plan favor?

5. Which states does the New Jersey Plan favor?

6. Make your predictions about state votes on the chart.

June 19: Should the Articles of Confederation be revised and amended? (Should we use the New Jersey Plan?)						
State	Yes		No		Divided	
	Prediction	Actual	Prediction	Actual	Prediction	Actual
Massachusetts						
Connecticut						
New York						
New Jersey						
Delaware						
Pennsylvania						
Maryland						
Virginia						
North Carolina						
South Carolina						
Georgia						

7. **Update the chart to reflect how states actually voted.**
8. **What pattern do you see to this vote? What might explain the way states voted?**

Patterns	Explanations

9. **Why might states with large populations have voted for the New Jersey Plan?**

10. **What patterns do you see in the voting?**

Patterns	Explanations

11. **Why might states with small populations have voted for the Virginia Plan?**

Name: _____ Date: _____ Class: _____

Constitutional Convention: The Great Compromise – Student Answer Sheet
Directions: Use the ArcGIS Online map titled, "The Constitutional Convention," to answer the following questions.

1. Make your predictions about state votes on the chart.
2. Update the chart to reflect how the states actually voted.

June 11: Should all states have one vote in the Senate, regardless of size?						
State	Yes		No		Divided	
	Prediction	Actual	Prediction	Actual	Prediction	Actual
Massachusetts						
Connecticut						
New York						
New Jersey						
Pennsylvania						
Maryland						
Virginia						
Georgia						

3. What patterns do you see in how states voted? What might explain these votes?

Patterns	Explanations

4. Can you think of a reason why South Carolina might have voted no? Does it make sense that a small state would vote not to have equal representation in the Senate?

5. How many delegates would Delaware get?

6. How many delegates would Virginia get?

7. Make your predictions about state votes on the chart.
8. Update the chart to reflect how the states actually voted.

June 11: Should states have representation based on population in the Senate?						
State	Yes		No		Divided	
	Prediction	Actual	Prediction	Actual	Prediction	Actual
Massachusetts						
Connecticut						
New York						
New Jersey						
Pennsylvania						
Maryland						
Virginia						
Georgia						

9. What patterns do you see in how states voted? What might explain these votes?

Patterns	Explanations

10. Can you think of a reason why Connecticut might have voted for proportional representation? Does it make sense that a small state would vote for representation based on population?

11. Who benefits from states being equally represented in the Senate? Who does not benefit?

12. Do you think it's fair for very small numbers of people to make decisions for large numbers of people?

13. Do you think it's fair for people who live in small states to have very little decision-making power when compared to large states?

14. How can you make the legislative branch work for all states – no matter what size they are?

Name: _____ Date: _____ Class: _____

Constitutional Convention: The 3/5 Compromise – Student Answer Sheet

Directions: Use the ArcGIS Online map titled, "The Constitutional Convention," to answer the following questions?

1. Make your predictions about state votes on the chart.
2. Update the chart to reflect how the states actually voted.

July 10: Should slaves be equal to whites for the purposes of deciding representation in the House of Representatives?						
State	Yes		No		Divided	
	Prediction	Actual	Prediction	Actual	Prediction	Actual
Massachusetts						
Connecticut						
Rhode Island						
New Jersey						
Delaware						
Pennsylvania						
Maryland						
Virginia						
North Carolina						
South Carolina						
Georgia						

3. What patterns do you see in how states voted? What might explain these votes?

Patterns	Explanations

4. Can you think of a reason why Virginia and North Carolina might have voted the way they did?

5. Make your predictions about state votes on the chart.
6. Update the chart to reflect how the states actually voted.

July 10: Should slaves count as 3/5 of a person for the apportionment of representation?						
State	Yes		No		Divided	
	Prediction	Actual	Prediction	Actual	Prediction	Actual
Massachusetts						
Connecticut						
Rhode Island						
New Jersey						
Delaware						
Pennsylvania						
Maryland						
Virginia						
North Carolina						
South Carolina						
Georgia						

7. What patterns do you see in how states voted? What might explain these votes?

Patterns	Explanations

8. What might be driving Southern states to vote yes for this proposal?

9. Why do you think South Carolina is the only state to vote no? What is different about South Carolina than other slave-holding states?

10. How did competing interests play a large role in the development of the United States Constitution?

11. What were the major issues surrounding the development of the Constitution of the United States of America?

Constitutional Convention: United States, 1787 Answer Key

1. Which state has the highest total population? What is the population of that state? **Virginia; 821, 227**

2. Which state has the smallest population? What is the population of that state? **Delaware; 59,096**

3. List the states that have the 4 highest and 4 lowest population totals. **Highest: Virginia, Massachusetts, Pennsylvania, and North Carolina. Lowest: Delaware, Rhode Island, Georgia, and Vermont**

4. What states had fewer than 200,000 people? **New Jersey, New Hampshire, Vermont, Georgia, Rhode Island, and Delaware**

5. What patterns do you notice regarding major cities in 1790? What are some explanations for those patterns? **They are located along the coast and major waterways. Waterways allowed for easy access to transportation.**

6. What states had cities with more than 10,000 people? What is similar about their location? **Maryland, South Carolina, Massachusetts, Pennsylvania, and New York. Most are located in the North. All are located on or near a major waterway.**

7. Which state has the highest slave population? How many slaves are in that state? **Virginia; 305, 057**

8. Which state has the smallest slave population? How many slaves are in that state? **Vermont and Massachusetts have none.**

9. List the states that have the 4 highest and 4 lowest slave totals. **Highest: Virginia, Maryland, South Carolina and North Carolina. Lowest: New Hampshire, Rhode Island, Vermont and Massachusetts.**

10. Where are there more slaves? Why? **There are more slaves in the South. The economy in the South is agricultural and requires more labor.**

11. In which states do slaves make up 25% or more of the population? **Virginia, North Carolina, Maryland, South Carolina, and Georgia.**

12. Which states have more than 200,000 people and fewer than 100,000 slaves? **Massachusetts, Pennsylvania, New York, and Connecticut.**

13. How do you think the needs and wants of large states and small states might be similar? How might they be different? **Answers will vary, but may contain the following ideas: Similar: They all want to be fairly represented in government. Different: They have different ideas on what that looks like. Large states want proportional representation, small states want equal representation.**

14. How do you think the needs and wants of states with large numbers of slaves might be similar than states with a small number (or no) of slaves? How might they be different? **Answers will vary, but may contain the following ideas: Similar: They want to be fairly represented in government. Different: They have different ideas on how slaves should figure into that equation. States with slaves want to count them for the purposes of representation but do not want to pay taxes for them. States without slaves do not want to count them for the purposes of representation but do want slave owners to pay taxes for them.**

Constitutional Convention: New Jersey Plan vs. Virginia Plan Answer Key

1. Make your predictions about state votes on the chart. **Answers will vary**
2. After you've updated your ArcGIS map, update the chart to reflect how states actually voted. *Yes:* **Massachusetts, New York, Delaware, Virginia, North Carolina, South Carolina and Georgia;** *No:* **Connecticut;** *Divided:* **New York**
3. What pattern do you see to this vote? What might explain the way states voted? **Most states voted yes. Most of these states believed the Articles of Confederation were not working. This vote would have scrapped the Articles and created a new government.**

4. Which states does the Virginia Plan favor? **Big states**
5. Which states does the New Jersey Plan favor? **Small states**
6. Make your predictions about state votes on the chart. **Answers will vary**
7. Update the chart to reflect how states actually voted. *Yes:* **Connecticut, New York, Delaware, and New Jersey.** *No:* **Massachusetts, Pennsylvania, Virginia, North Carolina, South Carolina, and Georgia.** *Divided:* **Maryland.**
8. What pattern do you see to this vote? What might explain the way states voted? **Most states voted no against simply revising the Articles of Confederation.**
9. Why might states with large populations have voted for the New Jersey Plan? **Answers will vary.**
10. What patterns do you see in the voting? **Most large states voted to use the Virginia Plan.**
11. Why might states with small populations have voted for the Virginia Plan? **The small states who voted for the Virginia Plan were slave states and may have believed that in time, their population would grow and they would be better served by proportional representation.**

Constitutional Convention: The Great Compromise Answer Key
1. Make your predictions about state votes on the chart. **Answers will vary.**
2. Update the chart to reflect how the states actually voted. *Yes:* **New York, Connecticut, New Jersey, Delaware, and Maryland.** *No:* **Massachusetts, Pennsylvania, Virginia, North Carolina, South Carolina and Georgia**
3. What patterns do you see in how states voted? What might explain these votes? **Most large states voted no. States with larger populations believed they should have more power in the Senate. States with smaller populations believed representation should be equal.**
4. Can you think of a reason why South Carolina might have voted no? Does it make sense that a small state would vote not to have equal representation in the Senate? **Answers will vary. Keep in mind: South Carolina had a growing slave population.**
5. How many delegates would Delaware get? **1**
6. How many delegates would Virginia get? **16**
7. Make your predictions about state votes on the chart. **Answers will vary.**
8. Update the chart to reflect how the states actually voted. *Yes:* **Massachusetts, Connecticut, Pennsylvania, Virginia, North Carolina, South Carolina.** *No:* **New York, New Jersey, Delaware.** *Divided:* **Maryland**
9. What patterns do you see in how states voted? What might explain these votes? **The states with larger populations voted to have representation based on population in the Senate. This would give them more power in the Senate.**
10. Can you think of a reason why Connecticut might have voted for proportional representation? Does it make sense that a small state would vote for representation based on population? **Answers will vary.**

11. Who benefits from states being equally represented in the Senate? Who does not benefit? **Small states benefit. Large states do not.**
12. Do you think it's fair for very small numbers of people to make decisions for large numbers of people? **Answers will vary.**
13. Do you think it's fair for people who live in small states to have very little decision-making power when compared to large states? **Answers will vary.**
14. How can you make the legislative branch work for all states – no matter what size they are? **Answers will vary.**

Constitutional Convention: The 3/5 Compromise Answer Key

1. Make your predictions about state votes on the chart. **Answers will vary.**
2. Update the chart to reflect how the states actually voted. *Yes:* **Delaware, South Carolina, Georgia.** *No:* **Massachusetts, Connecticut, New Jersey, Pennsylvania, Maryland, Virginia, North Carolina.**
3. What patterns do you see in how states voted? What might explain these votes? The **only states that voted yes were small states with slaves. They needed as many people to count for purposes of representation as possible.**
4. Can you think of a reason why Virginia and North Carolina might have voted the way they did? **Both states already had very large populations without counting slaves.**
5. Make your predictions about state votes on the chart. **Answers will vary.**
6. Update the chart to reflect how the states actually voted. *Yes:* **Connecticut, Virginia, North Carolina, Georgia.** *No:* **Massachusetts, Pennsylvania, New Jersey, Delaware, Maryland, South Carolina.**
7. What patterns do you see in how states voted? What might explain these votes? **Most states voted no. Many northern states did not want to count slaves at all.**
8. What might be driving Southern states to vote yes for this proposal? **This proposal would give them more of an edge in Congress.**
9. Why do you think South Carolina is the only state to vote no? What is different about South Carolina than other slave-holding states? **Almost half of its population consisted of slaves. They needed to count their slaves as a whole person or their power would be greatly reduced.**

10. How did competing interests play a large role in the development of the United States Constitution? **Large states, small states, slave states and non-slave states had to compromise in order to create a government that protected their rights.**
11. What were the major issues surrounding the development of the Constitution of the United States of America? **Structure of the government, representation in that government and how to count slaves.**

Chapter 4
Territorial Expansion of the United States

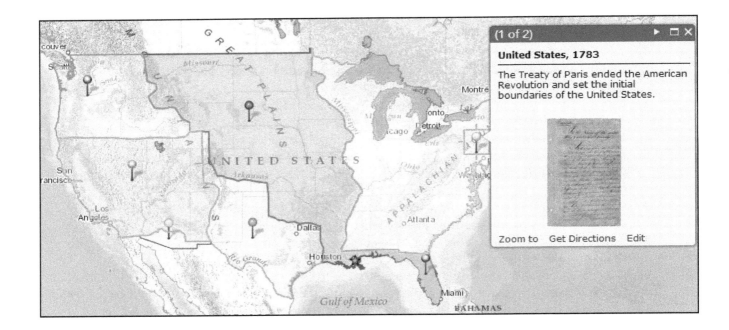

Territorial Expansion in the United States 1800-1850

Introduction

The student will understand how the United States expanded throughout the 19th century. Students will look at the acquisitions themselves, identify the area of the acquisition, the water systems added and the number of states created from each acquisition.

Teacher Information

Time

- Activity One: Treaty of Paris and the Louisiana Purchase
- Activity Two: Florida and Texas
- Activity Three: Oregon and California

Subjects
United States History

Level
Grades 5-12

Objectives
Students will be able to:

- Explain how each territory was acquired.
- Identify the states created and water systems added from each territorial acquisition
- Analyze a primary source related to each acquisition.

Spatial Thinking Fundamentals/Themes

- Location – location of new territories, river systems related to the territories and states located in each territory
- Region – areas of free states; areas of slave states;
- Comparison – how territories were acquired

Extension Activities

Have students write from a variety of perspectives to help them understand the territorial expansion of the United States.

Role	Audience	Format	Topic
US in 1783	France	persuasive letter	About that New Orleans...
France	United States	Response to request for New Orleans	You can have the city, but there's a catch...
United States	Spain	Memo	Send our slaves back from Florida
United States	Mexico	Threatening letter	For the last time, Texas' border is the Rio Grande
Manifest Destiny	Native Americans, Mexico, or History	Apology	It seemed like a good idea at the time
Britain	United States	Treaty request	We're tired of sharing Oregon
United States	Texas	Response to request for annexation	No more slave states.
United States	Texas	Response to request for annexation	Yes. The time is right!

Territorial Expansion: Treaty of Paris and the Louisiana Purchase - Instructions

Part I: The United States in 1783

1. Go to http://gisetc.com/mushago. Open the map, **Territorial Expansion.** Click **Modify Map.** You will be adding layers to the United States map to help you answer the questions.
2. **Click** the **Show Contents of Map** button so that all of the layers of the map become visible.

   Q1. **What body of water made up the western border of the United States in 1783?**

3. Hover over and **click** on the **United States 1783 layer.** Click on the **Show Table icon.**

   Q2. **Write down the details of how this territory became the United States.**
   Q3. **What was the total area of the United States in 1783?**

4. Close the table by clicking on the **Hide Table icon** ☒ .
5. **Click** on any river located on the United States 1783 map. Many of the rivers in this territory belong to a single river system.
   Q4. **What is the name of the largest river system located in the United States in 1783?**

6. Click on the light yellow map note located in the center of the extent of the United States in 1783. Follow the link inside this map note to the Library of Congress' webpage.

   Q5. **In addition to the United States and Britain, what other countries were involved in this conflict?**
   Q6. **What were two important provisions of the Treaty of Paris?**

Part II: Louisiana Purchase

7. **Click** the **Show Contents of Map** button so that all of the layers of the map become visible.
8. **Click** the box next to the layer titled, **Louisiana Purchase.**
9. **Click** the box next to the layer titled, **New Orleans.**

   Q7. **Where is New Orleans located? Why might this have been an important port city for the United States?**
   Q8. **What observations can you make about the Louisiana Purchase?**

10. Hover over and click on the **Louisiana Purchase** layer. Click on the **Show Table icon.**

    Q9. **How did the Louisiana Purchase become part of the United States?**
    Q10. **What was the total area of the Louisiana Purchase? What does this acquisition do to the size of the United States?**
    Q11. **How many states or parts of states were created from the Louisiana Purchase?**

11. Close the table by clicking on the **Hide Table icon** ☒ .
12. Click on the layer name **Major Rivers, click** on the **Filter icon.**
13. Inside the Filter window **create a filter** that will display features in the Major Rivers layer that match the expression "**SYSTEM is MISSISSIPPI.**"

    Q12. **What is the name of the largest river system in the Louisiana Purchase?**

Q13. Why would the addition of so many more miles of navigable river have been important to the United States during this time period?

14. **Click** on the map note located in the center of the Louisiana Purchase. Follow the link inside this map note to the Library of Congress' webpage.

Q14. What was Thomas Jefferson's fear if France took control of the port of New Orleans?

Q15. Why did Napoleon agree to sell the Louisiana Purchase to the United States?

Territorial Expansion: Florida and Texas - Instructions

Part I: Florida

1. Go to http://gisetc.com/mushago. Open the map, **Territorial Expansion.** Click **Modify Map.**
2. In front of you is a map of the United States. You will be adding layers to help you answer the questions.
3. **Click** the **Show Contents of Map** button so that all of the layers of the map become visible.

   Q1. Consider that slaves would often run away from bordering states. Many Native American tribes located in Florida would not return them to their owners. What observations can you make about Florida?

4. Click on the layer named **Florida** and **click on Show Table.**

   Q2. How did Florida become part of the United States?
   Q3. What was the total area of the Florida?
   Q4. How many states or parts of states were created from the acquisition of Florida?

5. Close the table by clicking on the **Hide Table icon** ☒.
6. Click on the map note located in the middle of Florida. Follow the link inside this map note to the Library of Congress' webpage. Scroll down the page. Read the paragraph entitled "U.S. Acquires Florida." (This is approximately five maps from the end of the list.)

   Q5. In addition to setting the price for Florida, what was another issue that needed to be settled between Spain and the United States?

Part II: Texas

7. **Click** the box next to the **Texas** layer.

   Q6. What observations can you make about Texas?

8. Hover over and click on the **Texas** layer. **Click** on the **Show Table icon.**

   Q7. How did Texas become part of the United States?
   Q8. What was the total area of Texas?
   Q9. How many states or parts of states were created from the acquisition of Texas?

9. Close the table by clicking on the **Hide Table icon** ☒.
10. **Turn on** the **Rivers layer. Click** on the **rivers** located **in Texas.** (If you can't see rivers in Texas, remember to clear the filter.)

    Q10. What are the names of the two river systems in the Texas?

11. Click on the map note located in the middle of Texas. Follow the link inside this map note to the Library of Congress' webpage.

    Q11. When did Texas gain its independence from Mexico?
    Q12. Why was Texas not admitted into the United States after its first request?

Territorial Expansion: Oregon and California - Instructions

Part I: Oregon

1. **Go to** http://gisetc.com/mushago. **Open** the map, **Territorial Expansion.** Click **Modify Map.**
2. In front of you is a map of the United States. You will be adding layers to help you answer the questions. **Click** the **Show Contents of Map** button so that all of the layers of the map become visible.
3. **Turn on** ☑ the layer, **Oregon.**

   Q1.   What observations can you make about Oregon?

4. Hover over and click on the **Oregon** layer. Click on the **Show Table icon.**

   Q2.   How did Oregon become part of the United States?
   Q3.   What was the total area of Oregon?
   Q4.   How many states or parts of states were created from the acquisition of Oregon?

5. Close the table by clicking on the **Hide Table icon** ☒ .
6. **Click** on the rivers located in Oregon.

   Q5.   What is the name of the largest river system in Oregon?

7. Click on the map note located in the middle of Oregon. Follow the link inside this map note to the Library of Congress' webpage.

   Q6.   What were some reasons Peter Burnett gave for traveling to Oregon?

Part IV: California

8. **Turn on** ☑ the layer, **California**

   Q7.   What observations can you make about California?

9. Hover over and click on the **California** layer. Click on the **Show Table icon.**

   Q8.   How did California become part of the United States?
   Q9.   What was the total area of California?
   Q10.   How many states or parts of states were created from the acquisition of California?

10. Close the table by clicking on the **Hide Table icon** ☒ .
11. **Click** on the rivers located in California.

   Q11.   What is the name of the largest river system in California?

12. Click on the map note located in the center of California. Follow the link inside this map note to the Library of Congress' webpage.

   Q12.   What led to the Mexican-American war?
   Q13.   What were the provisions (what did each side get) of the Treaty of Guadalupe-Hidalgo?

Name: _____ Date: _____ Class: _____

Treaty of Paris to Louisiana Purchase – Student Answer Sheet

Directions: Use the ArcGIS Online map titled, "Territorial Expansion" to answer the following questions.

1. Write down the details of how this territory became the United States.

2. What was the total area of the United States in 1783?

3. What is the name of the largest river system located in the United States in 1783?

4. In addition to the United States and Britain, what other countries were involved in this conflict?

5. What were two important provisions of the Treaty of Paris?

6. Where is New Orleans located? Why might this have been an important port city for the United States?

7. What observations can you make about the Louisiana Purchase?

8. How did the Louisiana Purchase become part of the United States?

9. What was the total area of the Louisiana Purchase? What does this acquisition do to the size of the United States?

10. How many states or parts of states were created from the Louisiana Purchase?

11. What is the name of the largest river system in the Louisiana Purchase?

12. Why would the addition of so many more miles of navigable river have been important to the United States during this time period?

13. What was Thomas Jefferson's fear if France took control of the port of New Orleans?

14. Why did Napoleon agree to sell the Louisiana Purchase to the United States?

Name: _____ Date: _____ Class: _____

Florida and Texas – Student Answer Sheet

Directions: Use the ArcGIS Online map titled, "Territorial Expansion" to answer the following questions.

1. What observations can you make about Florida? Consider that slaves would often run away from bordering states. Many Native American tribes located in Florida would not return them to their owners.

2. How did Florida become part of the United States?

3. What was the total area of the Florida?

4. How many states or parts of states were created from the acquisition of Florida?

5. In addition to setting the price for Florida, what was another issue that needed to be settled between Spain and the United States?

6. What observations can you make about Texas?

7. How did Texas become part of the United States?

8. What was the total area of the Texas?

9. How many states or parts of states were created from the acquisition of Texas?

10. What are the names of the two river systems in the Texas?

11. When did Texas gain its independence from Mexico?

12. Why was Texas not admitted into the United States after its first request?

Name: _____ Date: _____ Class: _____

Oregon and California – Student Answer Sheet

Directions: Use the ArcGIS Online map titled, "Territorial Expansion" to answer the following questions.

1. What observations can you make about Oregon?

2. How did Oregon become part of the United States?

3. What was the total area of Oregon?

4. How many states or parts of states were created from the acquisition of Oregon?

5. What is the name of the largest river system in Oregon?

6. What were some reasons Peter Burnett gave for traveling to Oregon?

7. What observations can you make about California?

8. How did California become part of the United States?

9. What was the total area of California?

10. How many states or parts of states were created from the acquisition of California?

11. What led to the Mexican-American War?

12. What were the provisions of the Treaty of Guadalupe-Hidalgo?

Treaty of Paris to Louisiana Purchase Answer Key

1. Write down the details of how this territory became the United States. **As a result of the Treaty of Paris, the United States became its own country.**
2. What was the total area of the United States in 1783? **843,255 square miles.**
3. What is the name of the largest river system located in the United States in 1783? **Mississippi River System**
4. In addition to the United States and Britain, what other countries were involved in this conflict? **France, Spain, and the Netherlands.**
5. What were two important provisions of the Treaty of Paris? **British recognition of the United States' independence and what its borders were.**
6. Where is New Orleans located? Why might this have been an important port city for the United States? **It is located at the mouth of the Mississippi River. It would give the United States control of the river.**
7. What observations can you make about the Louisiana Purchase? **Answers will vary.**
8. How did the Louisiana Purchase become part of the United States? **It was purchased from France for $15 million.**
9. What was the total area of the Louisiana Purchase? What does this acquisition do to the size of the United States? **891,405 square miles. It doubled the size of the United States.**
10. How many states or parts of states were created from the Louisiana Purchase? **14**
11. What is the name of the largest river system in the Louisiana Purchase? **Mississippi River System**
12. Why would the addition of so many more miles of navigable river have been important to the United States during this time period? **It allowed for more settlement and trade.**
13. What was Thomas Jefferson's fear if France took control of the port of New Orleans? **He feared the settlers in the Mississippi River Valley would lose free access to the port of New Orleans.**
14. Why did Napoleon agree to sell the Louisiana Purchase to the United States? **He needed the money and had suffered a recent military defeat in Haiti.**

Florida and Texas Answer Key

1. What observations can you make about Florida? Consider that slaves would often run away from bordering states. Many Native American tribes located in Florida would not return them to their owners. **Answers will vary.**
2. How did Florida become part of the United States? **The Adams-Onis Treaty. The United States agreed to pay American claims against the Spanish government for up to $5 million.**
3. What was the total area of the Florida? **58,666**
4. How many states or parts of states were created from the acquisition of Florida? **1**
5. In addition to setting the price for Florida, what was another issue that needed to be settled between Spain and the United States? **The southern and western borders of the Louisiana Purchase.**
6. What observations can you make about Texas? **Answers will vary.**
7. How did Texas become part of the United States? **It was annexed.**
8. What was the total area of the Texas? **389,752**
9. How many states or parts of states were created from the acquisition of Texas? **6**
10. What are the names of the two river systems in the Texas? **Mississippi and Rio Grande River Systems**

11. When did Texas gain its independence from Mexico? **1836**
12. Why was Texas not admitted into the United States after its first request? **Congress was not willing to admit another state that supported slavery.**

Oregon and California Answer Key

1. What observations can you make about Oregon? **Answers will vary.**
2. How did Oregon become part of the United States? **A treaty with Great Britain.**
3. What was the total area of Oregon? **285,336 square miles**
4. How many states or parts of states were created from the acquisition of Oregon? **4**
5. What is the name of the largest river system in Oregon? **Columbia River System**
6. What were some reasons Peter Burnett gave for traveling to Oregon? **He wanted to be a part of a great American community. He also believed it might cure his wife.**
7. What observations can you make about California? **Answers will vary.**
8. How did California become part of the United States? **The Treaty of Guadalupe-Hidalgo, ending the Mexican-American War.**
9. What was the total area of California? **527,122 square miles**
10. How many states or parts of states were created from the acquisition of California? **7**
11. What led to the Mexican-American War? **A dispute over Texas and its borders.**
12. What were the provisions of the Treaty of Guadalupe-Hidalgo? **Mexico had to cede 55% of its territory to the US in exchange for $15 million. It set the border of the US at the Rio Grande and called for the protection of Mexican nationals living within its border. The US promised to patrol its side of the border and it required arbitration if there were an issue in the future.**

Chapter 5
Trails to Rails:
Early U.S. Settlement Patterns

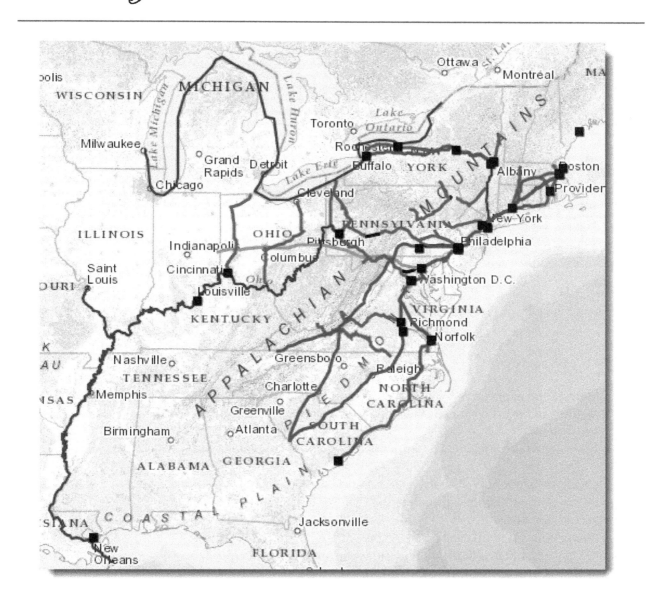

Trails to Rails

Introduction

The first half of the 19th century was a period of westward migration, settlement, and transportation experimentation. The year, 1850 marked a crossroads for US transportation. It was a peak for canal and steamboat transport, while railroads were being built at a furious pace. During this activity students use ArcGIS Online to predict, observe, and analyze the relationships between early American settlement patterns with the evolution of transportation networks.

Teacher Information

Time

- Activity One – Roads and Rivers: 1790 - 1810 – 45 Minutes
- Activity Two – Locks and Gauges: 1830 - 1850 – 45 Minutes

Subjects

United States History

Level

Grades 5-12

Objectives

Students will be able to:

- Identify and explain the relationship between bodies of water and human settlement
- Identify and explain some of the impacts that the new forms of transportation had on settlement
- Explain how the Erie Canal contributed to the rise of cities along the Great Lakes

Spatial Thinking Fundamentals/Themes

- Location – students will analyze the relative location of cities
- Interaction – students will analyze the relationship between emerging transportation options and settlement
- Movement – students will observe how settlement and transportation moved west and inland
- Region- students will observe how cities clustered in New England

Extensions

Encourage students to examine http://www.eriecanal.org/ or http://www.albanyinstitute.org/building-the-erie-canal.html for additional information. Students can add information to the map using map notes, create a web quest or they can create a presentation in a different medium about the impact of the Erie Canal and the steamboat.

Another site that is ripe for exploration is the University of Nebraska's digital history project, *Railroads and the Making of Modern America* (http://railroads.unl.edu/). This website contains a variety of topics, case studies, primary sources, and maps that pertain to the rise of railroads in the United States. Sample topics include: Slavery and Southern Railroads, Railroad Work and Workers, the 1877 Railroad Strike, The Civil War and Strategy, Politics and Corruption, and many more. Students could use this site to research and add information to the trails to rails maps using map notes, or you could assign students one of the topics to design a presentation or poster to share with the class.

Roads and Rivers: 1790 – 1810 Instructions

Part I: America in 1790
Complete this step prior to opening the ArcGIS Online map.

Consider and **answer questions #1 and #2** on the answer sheet:

> **Q1.** What are some of the landforms and climates that tend to attract people to settle?
>
> **Q2.** What is attractive about these landforms and climates?

You will be using ArcGIS Online to complete activities that will investigate how cities grew in the United States from 1790 – 1850. Using what you know about early US History make a prediction for where the first cities, according to the US Census were located in 1790. Write down your prediction on your answer sheet for **question #3.**

> **Q3.** Predict where the first cities were located in 1790?

1. Go to http://gisetc.com/mushago. Open the map, **Trails to Rails. Click** on **Modify Map.**

2. Compare your predictions to the settlement patterns you see on this map. **Complete the chart for question #4** while reflecting on these questions:
   Q4. Questions to Ponder:
   - How accurate were your predictions?
   - Where are cities located? Where are cities not located?
   - What patterns do you notice?
   - Do you have any questions about the patterns you see?

Find out what the three most populated cities were in 1790. To do this:

3. Hover over and click on the **Cities, 1790** layer. Click on the **Show Table** icon.

4. Click on the attribute field POP_1790 and choose **Sort Descending.**

ᴬ↓	Sort Ascending
ᶻ↓	Sort Descending
Σ	Statistics

5. Use this information to **answer questions #5 and #6** on the answer sheet.

> **Q5.** What were the 3 most populated cities in 1790 and what were their populations?

6. Click on the attribute field POP_1790 and choose **Statistics.** Use this information to answer question #6 on the answer sheet.

> **Q6.** What was the average population for the 24 major cities in 1790?

7. Close the table for Major Cities, 1790 by clicking on the **hide table icon** ☒

8. Turn on ☑ the layer Transportation, 1790 visible. Look at the map you have now and then **answer questions #7 and #8** on your answer sheet.

Q7. What are some observations you notice transportation options in 1790? Consider these questions:
- What were your transportation options?
- Where did the transportation routes go? Not go?
- What patterns do you see? Is there is a certain direction the networks travel?

Q8. What relationships do you see between settlement patterns and transportation in 1790?

9. Use the **measuring tool** to help you **answer questions #9 and #10**. To do this:

10. **Activate the Measure tool** by clicking on the word "Measure" at the top of your map.
11. Choose to measure a distance and **set the unit type to "Miles."** When you are finished, your measure window should look like the image to the right.
12. Use this tool to measure the distance that the city located farthest inland is from the coast. **Answer questions #9 and #10.**

Q9. Which city is farthest from the coast?
Q10. How far away is it?

13. Close the measurement window and look at the map to answer question #11.

Q11. What transportation options did people living in The United States have in 1790?

Part II: America in 1810

14. Turn on ☑ the layer, **Major Cities, 1810.** Compare the settlement pattern of cities in 1810 to the settlement pattern of cities in 1790. Compare your predictions to the settlement patterns you see on this map. **Complete the chart for question #1** while reflecting on these questions:

Q12. Questions to ponder:
- Where are cities located? Where are cities not located?
- What patterns do you notice?
- How does the distribution of the major cities in 1810 compare to the distribution of cities in 1790?
- What questions could you ask about the patterns you see?

Find out what the three most populated cities were in 1810. To do this:

15. Hover over and click on the **Cities, 1810** layer. Click on the **Show Table** icon.
16. Click on the attribute field POP_1810 and choose **Sort Descending.** Use this information to **answer question #2** on the answer sheet.

Q13. What were the 3 most populated cities in 1810 and what were their populations?

17. Click on the attribute field POP_1810 and choose **Statistics.** Use this information to **answer question #3** on the answer sheet.

Q14. What was the average population of the top 30 cities in 1810?

18. Close the table for Major Cities, 1810 by clicking on the **hide table icon** ☒

19. Turn on ☑ the layer, Transportation Improvements, 1810. Look at the map you have now and then **answer questions #4 and #5** on your answer sheet.

   Q15.   What are some observations you notice about transportation options in 1810?
   - **What were the transportation options?**
   - **Where did the transportation routes go? Not go?**
   - **What patterns do you see? Is there is a certain direction the networks travel?**
   - **What new types of transportation are visible in 1810?**

   Q16.   What relationships do you see between settlement patterns and transportation in 1810?

Use the **measuring tool** to help you answer questions #17and #18. To do this:

20. **Activate** the **Measure** tool. Click on the word "Measure" at the top of your map.
21. Choose to measure a distance and set the unit type to "Miles."
22. Use this tool to measure the distance that the city located farthest inland is from the coast. **Complete questions #17 and #18.**

   Q17.   Which city is farthest from the coast?
   Q18.   How far away was the farthest city from the coast in 1810?

23. Close the Measure window and look at the map to **answer question 19.**

   Q19.   What transportation options did people living in The United States have in 1810?

Locks and Gauges: 1830 – 1850 Instructions

Part I: America in 1830

1. **Turn on** ☑ the layer, **Major Cities 1830**. Compare the settlement pattern of cities in 1830 to the settlement pattern of cities in 1810. **Complete the chart for question #1 while reflecting on these questions:**

   Q1. Questions to ponder:
   - **Where are cities located? Where are cities not located?**
   - **What patterns do you notice?**
   - **How does the distribution of the major cities in 1830 compare to the distribution of cities in 1810?**
   - **What questions could you ask about the patterns you see?**

Let's find out what the three most populated cities were in 1830. To do this:

2. Hover over and click on the **Cities, 1830** layer. Click on the **Show Table** icon.

3. Click on the attribute field POP_1830 and choose **Sort Descending.** Use this information to **answer question #2 on the answer sheet.**

   Q2.   What were the 3 most populated cities in 1830 and what were their populations?

4. Click on the attribute field POP_1830 and choose **Statistics.** Use this information to **answer question #3 on the answer sheet.**

   Q3.   What was the average population of the top 30 cities in 1830?

5. Close the table for Major Cities, 1830 by clicking on the **hide table icon** ☒

6. Turn on ☑ the layer, Transportation, 1830. Look at the map you have now and then **answer questions #4 and #5 on your answer sheet.**

   Q4.   What are some observations you notice about types of transportation options in 1830? How do these options compare to 1810?
   Consider these questions:
   - **What were the transportation options?**
   - **Where did the transportation routes go? Not go?**
   - **What patterns do you see? Is there is a certain direction the networks travel?**
   - **Are there any new types of transportation emerging in 1830?**

   Q5. What relationships do you see between settlement patterns and transportation in 1830?

7. Use the **Measure tool** to locate and measure the city that was located farthest from the coast in 1830. To do this:

8. Activate the measuring tool click on the word "measure" at the top of your map.

9. Choose to measure a distance and set the unit type to "miles." When you are done your measure window should look like the image below.

10. Use this tool to measure the distance that the city located farthest inland from the coast. **Complete questions #6 and #7.**

> **Q6.** **Which city is farthest from the coast?**
> **Q7.** **How far away is it?**

Next, let's use the **Filter** command to find out how many of the major cities in 1830 were "canal cities" and/or "rail cities." To do this:

11. Hover over and click on the **Major Cities, 1830** layer. Click on the **Filter icon.**
12. Inside the **Filter** window create a filter that will display features in the Major Cities, 1830 layer that match the expression **NEARCANAL is Yes**
13. Choose **Apply Filter**
14. Show the table of filtered results by clicking the **Show Table icon**. Use this table and the new map to **answer question #8.**

> **Q8.** **How many cities in 1830 had access to a canal? What geographic patterns do you notice about these cities?**

15. Use the same steps that you used earlier to find out which 1830 cities had access to a railroad. The only change will be in the Filter command. This time create a filter that will display features in the Major Cities, 1830 layer that match the expression **NEAR_RAIL is Yes.** Use the results from this filter (table and map) to **answer question #9.**

> **Q9. How many cities in 1830 had access to a canal? What geographic patterns do you notice about these cities?**

16. Remove all filters inside the Filter window and then **answer question #10.**

> **Q10. What transportation options did people living in The United States have in 1830?**

Part II: America in 1850
Compare the settlement pattern of cities in 1850 to the settlement pattern of cities in 1830.

17. Turn on ☑ the layer, **Major Cities, 1850. Complete the chart for question 11 while reflecting on these questions:**

> **Q11.** **Questions to ponder:**
> - **Where are cities located? Where are cities not located?**
> - **What patterns do you notice?**
> - **How does the distribution of the major cities in 1850 compare to the distribution of cities in 1830?**
> - **What questions could you ask about the patterns you see?**

Let's find out what the three most populated cities were in 1850. To do this:

18. Hover over and click on the **Cities, 1850 layer**. Click on the **Show Table icon.**
19. Click on the attribute field POP_1850 and choose **Sort Descending.**

Use this information to **answer question #12** on the answer sheet as you did in the previous activity.

> **Q12.** **What were the 3 most populated cities in 1850 and what were their populations?**

20. Click on the attribute field POP_1850 and choose **Statistics**. Use this information to **answer question #13** on the answer sheet.

> **Q13.** **What was the average population of the top 30 cities in 1850?**

21. Close the table for Major Cities, 1850 by clicking on the **hide table icon** ☒

22. Turn on ☑ the layer, Transportation, 1850. Look at the map you have now and then **answer questions #14 and #15** on your answer sheet.

> **Q14.** **What are some observations you notice about types of transportation options in 1850? How do these options compare to 1830?**
> **Consider these questions:**
> - **What were the transportation options?**
> - **Where did the transportation routes go? Not go?**
> - **What patterns do you see? Is there is a certain direction the networks travel?**
> - **Are there any new types of transportation emerging in 1850?**

> **Q15.** **What relationships do you see between settlement patterns and transportation in 1850?**

Use the **Measure tool** to locate and measure the city that was located farthest from the coast in 1850. To do this:

23. Activate the Measure tool by clicking on the word "**Measure**" at the top of your map.
24. Choose to measure a distance and set the unit type to "Miles."
25. Use this tool to measure the distance that the city located farthest inland from the coast. **Complete questions #16 and #17.**

> **Q16.** **Which city is farthest from the coast?**
> **Q17.** **How far away is the farthest city from the coast in 1850?**

Next, let's use the **Filter** command to find out how many of the major cities in 1850 were "canal cities" and/or "rail cities." To do this:

26. Hover over and click on the **Major Cities, 1850** layer. Click on the **Filter** icon.
27. Inside the **Filter** window create a filter that will display features in the Major Cities, 1830 layer that match the expression **NEARCANAL is Yes**
28. Choose **Apply Filter**
29. Show the table of filtered results by clicking the **Show Table** icon below the layer **Major Cities, 1850.** Use this table and the new map to **answer question #18.**

> **Q18.** **How many cities in 1850 had access to a canal? What geographic patterns do you notice about these cities?**

30. Use the same steps you used earlier to find out which 1850 cities had access to a railroad. The only change will be Filter command. This time create a filter that will display features in the Major Cities, 1850 layer that match the expression **NEAR_RAIL is Yes.**

Use the results from this filter (table and map) to **answer question #19.**

> **Q19.** **How many cities in 1850 had access to a railroad? What geographic patterns do you notice about these cities?**

31. Remove all filters.

Let's see if there were any cities in 1850 that did not have access to a canal or a railroad. To do this:

32. Inside the Filter window create a multiple expression filter that will display features in the Major Cities 1850 layer that meet ANY of the following expressions:
    NEARCANAL is No
    NEAR _RAIL is No
33. Choose Apply. **Answer question #20** on your answer sheet.

> **Q20. Which cities did not have access to a railroad or a canal in 1850?**

Name: _____   Date: _____

Roads and Rivers: 1790 – 1810   Student Answer Sheet
The Beginning:

1. What are some of the landforms and climates that attract people to settle? _____

    _____

2. Why do they attract people? _____

    _____

3. *Make a prediction.* Where do you think cities will be located in 1790? _____

    _____

1790

4. *Check your prediction and complete the chart below.*

1790 Cities	
Observations	1. 2. 3.

5. What were the 3 most populated cities in 1790 and what were their populations?

RANK	CITY	POPULATION
1		
2		
3		

6. What was the average population for a major city in 1790?

7. *Turn on the layer for Transportation, 1790. Answer the questions below.*

1790 Transportation	
Observations	1. 2. 3.

8. *Analyze the information.*

1790: Making Connections	
What relationships do you see between settlement patterns and transportation in 1790?	

9. Which city is farthest from the coast?

10. How far away is it?

11. What transportation options do people have during this time period?

1810

12. *Turn on the layer Cities, 1810. Record your observations*

1810 Cities	
Observations	1. 2. 3.

13. What were the 3 most populated cities in 1810 and what were their populations?

RANK	CITY	POPULATION
1		
2		
3		

14. What was the average population for a major city in 1810?

15. *Turn on the layer for transportation. Answer the questions below.*

1810 Transportation	
Observations	1. 2. 3.

16. *Analyze the information.*

1810: Making Connections	
What relationship seems to exist between the invention of the steamboat and settlement in 1810?	
Compare the 1810 settlement and transportation layers to the 1790 settlement and transportation layers. **What differences do you notice?**	

17. Which city is farthest from the coast?

18. How far away is it?

19. What transportation options did people have during this time period?

Name: _____   Date: _____

Locks and Gauges: 1830 – 1850 Student Answer Sheet
1830

1. *Turn on the layer, 1830 Cities. Answer the questions below.*

1830 Cities	
Observations	1. 2. 3.

2. What were the 3 most populated cities in 1810 and what were their populations?

RANK	CITY	POPULATION
1		
2		
3		

3. What was the average population for a major city in 1830?

4. *Turn on the layer for transportation. Answer the questions below.*

1830 Transportation	
Observations	1. 2. 3.

5. *Analyze the information.*

1830: Making Connections	
What relationship exists between settlement and transportation in 1830?	
Compare the 1830 settlement and transportation layers to the 1810 settlement and transportation layers. **What differences do you notice? Similarities?**	

6. Which city is farthest from the Atlantic Ocean?

7. How far away is it?

8. How many major cities are located near canals?

9. How many major cities are located near railroads?

1850

10. *Turn on the layer 1850 cities. Answer the questions below.*

1850 Cities	
Observations	1. 2. 3.

11. What were the 3 most populated cities in 1850 and what were their populations?

RANK	CITY	POPULATION
1		
2		
3		

12. What was the average population for a major city in 1850?

13. *Turn on the layer for transportation. Answer the questions below.*

1850 Transportation	
Observations	1. 2. 3.

14. *Analyze the information.*

1850: Making Connections	
What relationship exists between the development of the railroads and where people are settling?	
Compare the 1850 settlement and transportation layers to the 1830 settlement and transportation layers. What differences do you notice? Similarities?	

15. Which city is farthest from the Atlantic Ocean?

16. How far away is it?

17. How many major cities are located near canals?

18. How many major cities are located near railroads?

19. Which major cities did not have access to a railroad or a canal in 1850?

Putting it all together

20. How did advancements in technology impact the settlement of the United States between 1790 and 1850?

Roads and Rivers: 1790 – 1810 Answer Key
The Beginning:

1. What are some of the landforms and climates that attract people to settle? **Answers will vary**

2. Why do they attract people? **Answers will vary**

3. *Make a prediction.* Where do you think cities will be located in 1790? **Answers will vary**

1790

4. *Check your prediction and complete the chart below.*

1790 Cities	
Observations	**Answers will vary. Key patterns include: coastal cities, mostly located in the coastal plains, more cities in the Middle and New England states.**

5. What were the 3 most populated cities in 1790 and what were their populations?

RANK	CITY	POPULATION
1	**NEW YORK**	**33,131**
2	**PHILADELPHIA**	**28,522**
3	**BOSTON**	**18,320**

6. What was the average population for a major city in 1790? **8,402**

7. *Turn on the layer for Transportation, 1790. Answer the questions below.*

1790 Transportation	
Observations	**Answers will vary. Possible observations include: Only roads were available (and rivers/ocean); Roads connect to the major cities; Roads follow valleys and/or hug the coast.**

8. *Analyze the information.*

1790: Making Connections	
What relationships do you see between settlement patterns and transportation in 1790?	**Answers will vary. Possible answers. Roads connected major cities. Settlement was limited as was transportation.**

9. Which city is farthest from the coast? **Albany, NY**

10. How far away is it? **110 – 120 miles**

11. What transportation options do people have during this time period? **Roads and navigable waterways (rivers, lakes, ocean)**

1810

12. *Turn on ☑ the layer Major Cities 1810. Record your observations*

1810 Cities	
Observations	**Answers will vary. Possible observations include: Pattern remains pretty much the same; A few new cities emerge near Washington, DC; Settlement still located between the mountains and the coast; New Orleans shows up due to the Louisiana Purchase in 1803.**

13. What were the 3 most populated cities in 1810 and what were their populations?

RANK	CITY	POPULATION
1	**NEW YORK**	**96,373**
2	**PHILADELPHIA**	**53,722**
3	**BALTIMORE**	**46,555**

14. What was the average population for a major city in 1810? **15,520**

15. *Turn on the layer for transportation. Answer the questions below.*

1810 Transportation	
Observations	**Answers will vary. Possible observations include: Same roads at 1790; A steamboat route appears along the Hudson River connecting Albany and New York City**

16. *Analyze the information.*

1810: Making Connections	
What relationship seems to exist between the invention of the steamboat and settlement in 1810?	**A new city appears outside of Albany, NY. 4 of the major cities are located along the Hudson river and the steamboat route.**
Compare the 1810 settlement and transportation layers to the 1790 settlement and transportation layers. **What differences do you notice?**	**The major difference the addition of the steamboat route in New York.**

17. Which city is farthest from the coast? **Schenectady, NY**

18. How far away is it? **140 – 150 miles**

19. What transportation options did people have during this time period? **Roads, navigable waterways, and limited access to the steamboat**

Locks and Gauges: 1830 – 1850 Answer Key
1830

1. *Turn on the layer, 1830 Cities. Answer the questions below.*

1830 Cities	
Observations	**Answers will vary. Possible observations include: Cities have moved inland; a number of cities are located between Albany and Lake Erie; Cities have moved into the Ohio Valley along the Ohio River.**

2. What were the 3 most populated cities in 1810 and what were their populations?

RANK	CITY	POPULATION
1	**NEW YORK**	**202,589**
2	**BALTIMORE**	**80,620**
3	**PHILADELPHIA**	**80,462**

3. What was the average population for a major city in 1830? **27,742**

4. *Turn on the layer for transportation. Answer the questions below.*

1830 Transportation	
Observations	**Answers will vary. Possible observations include: the transportation network is moving inland and west. Steamboat routes follow the great lakes, the Ohio River, and Mississippi River; Canals have also been built and are connecting cities to other bodies of water.**

5. *Analyze the information.*

1830: Making Connections	
What relationship exists between settlement and transportation in 1830?	**Cities and transportation are moving west and along the major waterways. A lot of options are emerging.**

Compare the 1830 settlement and transportation layers to the 1810 settlement and transportation layers. **What differences do you notice? Similarities?**	**Everything is moving west. People can now choose to travel by trail, steamboat, canals, or by way of the National road. There are a few railroads being built outside of Baltimore and Philadelphia.**

6. Which city is farthest from the coast? **Louisville, KY or Cincinnati, OH**

7. How far away is it? **540 – 570 miles**

8. How many major cities are located near canals? **23**

9. How many major cities are located near railroads? **5**

1850

10. *Turn on the layer 1850 cities. Answer the questions below.*

1850 Cities	
Observations	**Answers will vary. Possible observations include: Cities have reached the Great Lakes and the Mississippi River (St. Louis).**

11. *What were the 3 most populated cities in 1850 and what were their populations?*

RANK	CITY	POPULATION
1	**NEW YORK**	**515,547**
2	**BALTIMORE**	**169,054**
3	**BOSTON**	**136,881**

12. What was the average population for a major city in 1850? **72,189**

13. *Turn on the layer for transportation. Answer the questions below.*

1850 Transportation	
Observations	**Answers will vary. Possible observations include: Railroads show up all over the place, but mostly in the Northeast and Midwest.; Canals steamboat routes stay relatively unchanged**

14. *Analyze the information.*

1850: Making Connections	
What relationship exists between the development of the railroads and where people are settling?	**Railroads are being built where the people are. Mostly in the Northeast of the United States.**
Compare the 1850 settlement and transportation layers to the 1830 settlement and transportation layers. What differences do you notice? Similarities?	**Railroads are being built at a rapid pace. In many ways the Northern part of the country is cities, railroad, and canals are concentrated. More railroads are being built in the South than in 1830.**

15. Which city is farthest from the coast? **St. Louis MO**

16. How far away is it? **650 – 760 miles (depending on the way it is measured)**

17. How many major cities are located near canals? **24**

18. How many major cities are located near railroads? **29**

19. Which major cities did not have access to a railroad or a canal in 1850? **St. Louis, MO**

Putting it all together

20. How did advancements in technology impact the settlement of the United States between 1790 and 1850? **Answers will vary.**

Chapter 6
1860 Census: The Worlds of North and South

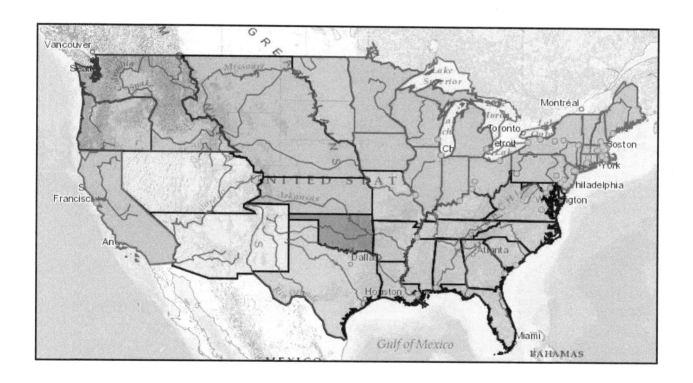

1860 Census: The Worlds of North and South

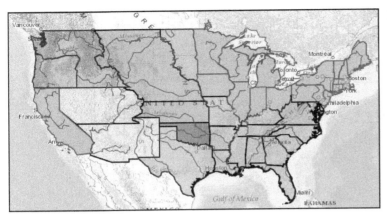

Introduction

This GIS investigation uses ArcGIS Online to explore the 1860 census to better understand the demographics and economies of Free States and Slave States. This includes an exploration of the population, slavery, basic and specific economic data by state and at the county level.

Teacher Information

Time

- Activity One – Population and Slavery by State – 30 minutes
- Activity Two – Slavery by County – 30 minutes
- Activity Three – Basic Economics by County – 30 minutes
- Activity Four – Detailed Economics by County – 30 minutes

Subjects

United States History

Level

Grades 5-12

Objectives

Students will be able to:

- Identify and explain the difference between Free States and Slave States
- Identify, compare and explain the economic differences between Free States and Slave States based on the Census of 1860
- Explain how slavery impacted the economy of Free States and Slave States

Spatial Thinking Fundamentals/Themes

- Location – Free States, Slave States
- Region – differing economies in free states and slave states
- Comparison – Manufacturing, agriculture, access to railroads, cotton value, labor costs

Extension Activities

Have students write an editorial or create a political cartoon for either the North or South using information learned from these lessons. Some topics might include: slavery, secession or the coming election of 1860.

1860 Census: Population and Slavery – Instructions

Part I: Population
1. Go to http://gisetc.com/mushago. Open the map, **Two Worlds of North and South**. Click **Modify Map**.

First let's create a thematic map of the United States based on population.

2. **Click** the **Show Contents of Map** button so that all of the layers of the map become visible.

In order to get an accurate map, we must first filter out some data.

3. **Hover** over and click on the **1860 State Census layer.** Click on the **Filter** icon.
4. Inside the Filter window create a filter that will exclude data that contains the expression -99 (which means no data) from the TOT_POP column located in the 1860_STATE_CENSUS layer.
   TOT_POP is not -99
5. Click **Apply Filter.**

Now we can create an accurate thematic map based on population.

6. Hover over and click on the **1860 State Census layer.** **Click** on the **Change Style** icon.
7. For **Choose an attribute to show** choose **TOT_POP.** Click on the **Options** tab under **Counts and Amounts (Color).**
   - Keep **Divided** at **None**
   - Click on the **Symbols** Ramp. Change the color ramp to Green.
   - **Check** the box next to **Classify Data**
   - Use **Natural Breaks**
   - With **5 classes**

8. Click **Done Changing Symbols.**

   Q1. **What patterns do you notice about the population distribution in 1860? Record your observations and questions.**

9. Show the table of filtered results by clicking the layer 1860 State Census and then clicking on the **Show Table** icon.

   Q2. **Which four states had the highest total population in 1860? (HINT: sort TOT_POP to display descending)**
   Q3. **Which four states had the lowest total population in 1860? (HINT: sort TOT_POP to display ascending)**

10. Hover over and click on the layer named 1860 State Census. Click on the **Filter icon** then **click Remove Filter.**

Part II: Slavery

Now let's take a look at slavery in the United States in 1860.

11. Hover over and click on the layer named **Civil War States**. Click on the **Filter icon**.
12. Inside the Filter window create a filter that will display features in the 1860 State Census layer that match the expression "FR_SLV_ST is FREE"

Q4.   In 1860, how many states were Free States?

13. Hover over and click on the layer named 1860 State Census. Click on the **Filter icon** then **click Remove Filter.**
14. Inside the Filter window create a filter that will display features in the 1860 State Census layer that match the expression "FR_SLV_ST is SLAVE."

Q5.   In 1860, how many states were Slave States? (Hint: Don't just count the states, use the table.)

Now let's create a thematic map based on slavery in the United States in 1860. In order to get an accurate map, we must first filter out some data.

15. Hover over and click on the layer named 1860 State Census. Click on the **Filter icon** and click **Remove Filter**.
16. Then, hover again over and click on the layer named 1860 State Census. Click on the **Filter icon.**
17. Inside the **Filter** window create a filter that will exclude data that contains the expression -99 (which means no data) from the TOT_SLVS column located in the 1860 State Census layer. (Do not apply the filter yet.)
18. At the top of the box, **click** the plus (**+**) sign to add another expression. Add the expression that says "TOT_SLVS is not 0."
19. You should have two lines in your filter window.
    TOT_SLVS is not -99
    TOT_SLVS is not 0

20. Choose **Apply Filter**.
21. Close the table window.

Now we can create an accurate thematic map based on slave population.

22. Hover over and click on the layer named 1860 State Census. **Click** on the **Change Style icon.**
23. For **Choose an attribute to show** choose TOT_SLVS. Click on the **Options** tab under **Counts and Amounts (Color)**.
    - Keep **Divided** at **None**
    - Click on the **Symbols** Ramp. Change the color ramp to Green.
    - **Check** the box next to **Classify Data**
    - Use **Natural Breaks**
    - With **5 classes**

24. **Click Done Changing Symbols.** Use the thematic map you have just created to answer question 6.

Q6. **What patterns do you notice about the slave population distribution in 1860? Record your observations and questions.**

25. Show the table of filtered results by clicking on the **Show Table icon** below the layer 1860 State Census.

Q7. **Which four states had the highest slave population in 1860? (HINT: sort TOT_SLV to display descending)**

26. Remove the **Filter** by clicking on the **Filter icon** and choosing **Remove Filter.**
27. Close the table by clicking on hide table.

Now you will look at the percentage of slaves in each state.

28. Inside the Filter window create a new filter that will exclude data that contains the expression -99 (which means no data) from the SLV_PCT column located in the 1860 State Census layer.
29. At the top of the box, **click** the plus (+) sign to add another expression. Add the expression that says "SLV_PCT is not 0." You'll have two rows in the filter.
SLV_PCT is not -99
SLV_PCT is not 0
30. Click **Apply Filter.**
31. Hover over and click on the layer named 1860 State Census. Click on the **Change Style icon.**
32. For **Choose an attribute to show** choose **SLV_PCT**. Click on the **Options** tab under **Counts and Amounts (Color)**.
    • Keep **Divided** at **None**
    • Click on the **Symbols** Ramp. Change the color ramp to Green.
    • **Check** the box next to **Classify Data**
    • Use **Natural Breaks**
    • With **5 classes**
33. Open the table by clicking on the **Show Table icon** for the 1860 State Census layer.

Q8. **Which four states had the highest percentage of its population comprised of slaves in 1860? (HINT: sort SLV_PCT to display descending)**
Q9. **Why do you think it is important to understand both the total number of slaves and percentage of slaves? Why might looking at just the total number of slaves be misleading?**

34. Hover over and click on the **1860 State Census** layer. Click on the **Filter icon** then **click Remove Filter.**

Part III: Cities
35. **Click** the **Show Contents of Map** button so that all of the layers of the map become visible.
36. **Click** the layer titled **1860 State Census**. Click on the **Show Legend** icon.
37. **Turn on** ☑ the layer titled Large Cities.

Q10. **What do you notice about the distribution of major cities (those with more than 20,000 people)?**

Let's find out how many major cities were located in slave states and Free states.

38. Hover over and click on the layer named **1860 State Census**. Click on the **Filter icon.**
39. Inside the Filter window **create a filter** that will display features in the **1860 State Census** layer that match the expression **FR_SLV_ST is SLAVE.**

   Q11. How many major cities were located in slave states?

40. Hover over and click on the layer named **1860 State Census.** Click on the **Filter icon** and **click** the tab labeled **Edit.**
41. Inside the Filter window change the filter to display features in the 1860 State Census layer that match the expression **FR_SLV_ST is FREE.**

   Q12. How many major cities were located in Free states?

1860 Census: Slavery by County – Instructions

Part I: Big Picture

1. Go to http://gisetc.com/mushago. Open the map, **Two Worlds of North and South**. Click **Modify Map**.

Let's create a thematic map based on the percentage of slaves in each county of the United States in 1860.

2. **Click** the **Show Contents of Map** button so that all of the layers of the map become visible.
3. **Turn off** ☐ the **1860 State Census** layer.
4. **Turn on** ☑ the **1860 County Census** layer.

In order to get an accurate map, we must first filter out some data.

5. Hover over and click on the layer named **1860 County Census**. **Click** on the **Filter icon**.
6. Inside the Filter window create a filter that will exclude data that contains the expression -99 (which means no data) **SLV_PCT is not -99** in the 1860 County Census layer.
7. At the top of the box, **click** the plus (**+**) sign to add another expression. Add the expression that says **PCT_SLV is not 0**.

8. Choose Apply Filter.

Now we can create an accurate thematic map based on the percentage of slaves in each county of the United States in 1860.

9. Hover over and click on the layer named **1860 County Census**. Click on the **Change Style icon.**
10. For **Choose an attribute to show** choose **SLV_PCT**. Click on the **Options** tab under **Counts and Amounts (Color)**.
    *   Keep **Divided** at **None**
    *   Click on the **Symbols** Ramp. Change the color ramp to Yellow to Brown.
    *   **Check** the box next to **Classify Data**
    *   Use **Natural Breaks**
    *   With **5 classes**
11. **Click Done Changing Symbols.**

    Q1. **What patterns do you notice about the distribution of slavery at the county level in 1860?**

12. Hover over and click on the layer named **1860 County Census**. Click on the **Filter icon** then **click Remove Filter.**

Part II: The Details

Now let's find out how many counties in the United States had a population that was more than 50% enslaved.

13. Hover over and click on the layer named **1860 County Census**. Click on the **Filter icon**.
14. Inside the Filter window create a filter that will display features in the 1860 County Census layer that match the expression "SLV_PCT is at least 50"

15. Choose **Apply Filter**.
16. Hover over and click the layer named **1860 County Census**. **Click** on the **Show Table icon**. Look at the top of the table where it says **features**.

> **Q2.** **How many counties in the United States had a total population that was comprised of more than 50% slaves?**

17. Hover over and click on the layer named **1860 County Census. Click** on the **Filter icon** and then **click** the **Edit tab.**
18. Using the same steps you just used, create filters to answer the following questions.

> **Q3.** **How many counties' population was comprised of more than 70% slaves?**
> **Q4.** **How many counties' population was comprised of more than 90% slaves?**

19. Hover over and click on the layer named 1860 County Census. **Click** on the **Filter icon,** and then **click** the **Edit tab.**
20. Inside the Filter window create a filter that will display features in the 1860 County Census layer that match the expression **SLVS_1 is at least 1**.
21. Choose **Apply Filter**.

> **Q5.** **How many counties had individuals who owned 1 or more slaves?**

22. Use the same steps to answer the following questions:

> **Q6.** **How many counties had individuals who owned 50 - 99 slaves? (SLVS_50_99)**
> **Q7.** **How many counties had individuals who owned 500 - 999 slaves? (SLVS_500_999)**
> **Q8.** **How many counties had individuals who owned 1000 or more slaves? (SLVS_1000OV)**

Let's find out how many slaves lived in Slave States and how many slaves lived in Free States.

23. Hover over and click on the layer named **1860 County Census**. Click on the **Filter icon**.
24. Inside the Filter window create a filter that will display features in the 1860 County Census layer that match the expression **FR_SLV is SLAVE.**
25. Choose **Apply Filter**.
26. Hover over and click on the layer named **1860 County Census. Click** on the **Show Table icon.**
27. **Click** on the column titled **TOT_SLVS**. Choose Statistics.

> **Q9.** **How many people were enslaved in slave counties?**

28. Hover over and click on the layer named **1860 County Census. Click** on the **Filter icon** and then **click** on the **Edit tab.**

29. Inside the Filter window create a filter that will display features in the 1860 County Census layer that match the expression "FR_SLV is FREE"
30. Choose **Apply Filter**.
31. Hover over and click on the layer named **1860 County Census**. **Click** on the **Show Table icon.**
32. **Click** on the column titled **TOT_SLVS**. Choose Statistics.

    Q10.   **How many people were enslaved in free counties?**

1860 Census: Economics by County – Instructions

Part I: Manufacturing

1. Go to http://gisetc.com/mushago. Open the map, **Two Worlds of North and South**. Click **Modify Map.**

Let's create a thematic map that shows manufacturing by county.

2. **Click** the **Show Contents of Map** button so that all of the layers of the map become visible.
3. **Turn on** ☑ the 1860 County Census layer.

In order to get an accurate map, we must first filter out some data.

4. Hover over and click on the layer named **1860 County Census. Click** on the **Filter icon**.
5. Inside the Filter window **create a filter** that will exclude data from counties where there was no manufacturing. Create an expression that says **MAN_PROD_1 is not 0.**
6. Choose **Apply Filter.**

Now we can create an accurate thematic map based on manufacturing value by county.

7. Hover over and click on the layer named **1860 County Census. Click** on the **Change Style icon.**
8. For **Choose an attribute to show** choose **MAN_PROD_1**. Click on the **Options** tab under **Counts and Amounts (Color).**
   - Keep **Divided** at **None**
   - Click on the **Symbols** Ramp. Change the color ramp to Yellow to Brown.
   - **Check** the box next to **Classify Data**
   - Use **Natural Breaks**
   - With **5 classes**

9. **Click Done Changing Symbols.**

   Q1.   **What patterns do you notice about manufacturing production in 1860 at the county level?**

10. Show the table of filtered results by clicking on the **Show Table icon** below the **1860 County Census** layer.

    Q2.   **What were the top four manufacturing counties in 1860? (HINT: Sort MAN_PROD_1 descending)**

11. Hover over and click on the layer named **1860 County Census. Click** on the **Filter icon** and then **click** on the **Edit tab.**
12. At the top of the box, **click** the plus (+) sign to Add another expression. Inside the Filter window create a filter that will display features in the **1860 County Census** layer that match the expression **FR_SLV is SLAVE.**
13. Choose **Apply Filter.**
14. Hover over and click on the layer named **1860 County Census. Click** on the **Show Table icon.**
15. **Click** on the column titled **MAN_PROD_1**. Choose **Statistics.**

Q3. **What was the total value of manufactured goods produced in slave counties?**

16. Once you have answered that question, repeat the process using **FR_SLV is FREE** as the filter.

Q4. **What was the total value of manufactured goods produced in free counties?**

17. Hover over and click on the layer named **1860 County Census**. **Click** on the **Filter icon** then **click Remove Filter.**

Part II: Labor Costs
Let's create a thematic map that shows labor costs by county.

18. **Click** the **Show Contents of Map** button so that all of the layers of the map become visible.
19. **Click** the layer titled **1860 County Census**.

In order to get an accurate map, we must first filter out some data.

20. Hover over and click on the layer named **1860 County Census**. **Click** on the **Filter icon**.
21. Inside the Filter window create a filter that will exclude data from counties where there was no labor costs. Create an expression that says **LABORCOST is not 0**.
22. Choose **Apply Filter**.

Now we can create an accurate thematic map based on labor costs by county.

23. Hover over and click on the layer named **1860 County Census**. **Click** on the **Change Style icon.**
24. For **Choose an attribute to show** choose **LABORCOST**. Click on the **Options** tab under **Counts and Amounts (Color)**.
    - Keep **Divided** at **None**
    - Click on the **Symbols** Ramp. Change the color ramp to Yellow to Brown.
    - **Check** the box next to **Classify Data**
    - Use **Natural Breaks**
    - With **5 classes**

25. **Click Done Changing Symbols.**
26. Use the thematic map you have just created to answer question 1.

Q5. **What patterns do you notice about labor costs at the county level in 1860?**

27. Show the table of filtered results by clicking the **Show Table icon** below the layer 1860 County Census.

Q6. **Which four counties had the highest labor costs in 1860? (HINT: Sort LABORCOST descending)**

28. Hover over and click on the layer named **1860 County Census**. **Click** on the **Filter icon** and then **click** the **Edit tab.**
29. At the top of the box, **click** the plus (**+**) sign to add another expression. Inside the Filter window create a filter that will display features in the **1860 County Census** layer that match the expression **FR_SLV is SLAVE**.
30. Choose **Apply Filter**.

31. Hover over and click on the layer named **1860 County Census**. **Click** on the **Show Table icon.**

32. **Click** on the column titled **LABORCOST**. Choose **Statistics.**

    Q7.   **What were the total labor costs in slave counties?**

33. Once you have answered that question, repeat the process using **FR_SLV is FREE** as the filter.

    Q8.   **What were the total labor costs in free counties?**

34. Hover over and click on the layer named 1860 County Census. **Click** on the **Filter** icon and then **click Remove Filter.**

1860 Census: Economic Detail by County – Instructions

Part I: Cotton Value

1. Go to http://gisetc.com/mushago. Open the map, **Two Worlds of North and South**. Click **Modify Map**.

Let's create a thematic map that shows cotton value by county.

2. **Click** the **Show Contents of Map** button so that all of the layers of the map become visible.
3. **Click** the layer titled **1860 County Census**.

In order to get an accurate map, we must first filter out some data.

4. Hover over and click on the layer named **1860 County Census. Click** on the **Filter icon**.
5. Inside the Filter window **create a filter** that will exclude data from counties where there was no cotton. Create an expression that says **COTTON_VAL is not 0**.
6. Choose **Apply Filter**.

Now we can create an accurate thematic map based on cotton value by county.

7. Hover over and click on the layer named **1860 County Census. Click** on the **Change Style icon**.
8. For **Choose an attribute to show** choose **COTTON_VAL**. Click on the **Options** tab under **Counts and Amounts (Color)**.
    *   Keep **Divided** at **None**
    *   Click on the **Symbols** Ramp.
    *   **Check** the box next to **Classify Data**
    *   Use **Natural Breaks**
    *   With **5 classes**
9. **Click Done Changing Symbols.**

    Q1.   What patterns do you notice about cotton value at the county level in 1860?

10. Show the table of filtered results by clicking on the Show Table icon below the layer **1860 County Census.**

    Q2.   What four counties had the highest cotton value in 1860? (HINT: Sort COTTON_VAL descending)

11. Hover over and click on the layer named **1860 County Census. Click** on the **Filter icon** and then **click** on the **Edit tab.**
12. At the top of the box, **click** the plus (+) sign to add another expression. Inside the Filter window create a filter that will display features in the **1860 County Census** layer that match the expression **FR_SLV is SLAVE.**
13. Choose **Apply Filter.**
14. Hover over and click on the layer named **1860 County Census. Click** on the **Show Table icon.**
15. **Click** on the column titled **COTTON_VAL.** Choose **Statistics.**

    Q3.   What was the total value of cotton in slave counties?

16. Once you have answered that question, repeat the process using **FR_SLV is FREE** as the filter.

> **Q4.** **What was the total value of cotton in free counties?**

17. Hover over and click on the layer named **1860 County Census**. Click on the **Filter icon** and then **click Remove Filter.**

Part II: Agricultural Value

Let's create a thematic map that shows agricultural value by county.

18. **Click** the layer titled **1860 County Census.**

In order to get an accurate map, we must first filter out some data.

19. Hover over and click on the layer named **1860 County Census. Click** on the **Filter icon.**
20. Inside the Filter window create a filter that will exclude data from counties where there was no manufacturing. Create an expression that says **AGR_VALUE is not 0**.
21. Choose **Apply Filter.**

Now we can create an accurate thematic map based on agricultural value by county.

22. Hover over and click on the layer named **1860 County Census. Click** on the **Change Style icon.**
23. For **Choose an attribute to show** choose **AGR_VALUE**. Click on the **Options** tab under **Counts and Amounts (Color).**
    - Keep **Divided** at **None**
    - Click on the **Symbols** Ramp. Change the color ramp to Yellow to Brown.
    - **Check** the box next to **Classify Data**
    - Use **Natural Breaks**
    - With **5 classes**
24. **Click Done Changing Symbols.**
25. Use the thematic map you have just created to answer question 1.

> **Q5.** **What patterns do you notice about agricultural value at the county level in 1860?**

26. Show the table of filtered results by clicking the **Show Table icon** below the layer 1860 County Census.

> **Q6.** **Which four counties had the highest agricultural value in 1860? (HINT: Sort AGR_VALUE descending)**

27. Hover over and click on the layer named **1860 County Census. Click** on the **Filter icon** and then **click** on the **Edit tab.**
28. At the top of the box, **click** the plus (**+**) sign to add another expression. Inside the Filter window create a filter that will display features in the **1860 County Census** layer that match the expression **FR_SLV is SLAVE.**
29. Choose **Apply Filter.**
30. Hover over and click on the layer named 1860 County Census. **Click** on the **Show Table icon.**
31. **Click** on the column titled **AGR_VALUE.** Choose Statistics.

Q7. **What was the total agricultural value in slave counties?**

32. Once you have answered that question, repeat the process using **FR_SLV is FREE** as the filter.

Q8. **What was the total agricultural value in free counties?**

33. Hover over and click on the layer named **1860 County Census**. **Click** on **Filter icon** then **click Remove Filter.**

Part III: Railroads
Let's create a thematic map that shows access to railroads by county.

34. **Click** the layer titled **1860 County Census**.
35. Hover over and click on the layer named **1860 County Census**. **Click** on the **Filter icon**.
36. Inside the Filter window create an expression that says **RAIL is 1**.
37. Choose **Apply Filter**.

Q9. **What patterns do you notice about access to railroads at the county level in 1860?**

38. Hover over and click on the layer named **1860 County Census**. Click on the **Filter icon** and then click on the **Edit tab.**
39. At the top of the box, **click** the plus (+) sign to add another expression. Inside the Filter window create a filter that will display features in the **1860 County Census** layer that match the expression **FR_SLV is SLAVE**.
40. Choose **Apply Filter**.
41. Hover over and click on the layer named **1860 County Census**. **Click** on the **Show Table icon**.
42. **Click** on the column titled **RAIL**. Choose **Statistics**.

Q10. **How many counties had access to a railroad in slave states in 1860?**

43. Once you have answered that question, repeat the process using **FR_SLV is FREE** as the filter.

Q11. **How many counties had access to a railroad in Free states in 1860?**

44. Hover over and click on the layer named 1860 County Census. **Click** on the **Filter icon** and then **click Remove Filter.**

Name: _____ Date: _____ Class: _____

Population and Slavery – Student Answer Sheet

Directions: Use the ArcGIS Online map titled The 1860 Census: The Worlds of North and South to answer the following questions.

1. What patterns do you notice about the population distribution 1860? Record your observations and questions.

Observations	Questions

2. Which four states had the highest total population in 1860?	3. Which four states had the lowest total population in 1860?

4. In 1860, how many states were Free States?	5. In 1860, how many states were Slave States?

6. What patterns do you notice about the slave population distribution in 1860? Record your observations and questions.

Observations	Questions

7. Which four states had the highest slave population in 1860?

State	Population

8. Which four states had the highest percentage of its population comprised of slaves in 1860?

State	Percentage

9. Why do you think it is important to understand both the total number of slaves and percentage of slaves? Why might looking at just the total number of slaves be misleading?

10. What do you notice about the distribution of major cities (those with more than 20,000 people)? Record your observations and questions.

Observations	Questions

11. How many major cities were located in slave states?

12. How many major cities were located in Free states?

Name: _____ Date: _____ Class: _____

Slavery by County – Student Answer Sheet

Directions: Use the ArcGIS Online map titled The 1860 Census: The Worlds of North and South to answer the following questions.

1. What patterns do you notice about the distribution of slavery at the county level in 1860?

Observations	Questions

2. How many counties in the United States had population that was comprised of more the 50% slaves?

3. How many counties' population was comprised of more than 70% slaves?

4. How many counties' population was comprised of more than 90% slaves?

5. How many counties had individuals who owned 1 or more slaves?

6. How many counties had individuals who owned 50 – 99 slaves?

7. How many counties had individuals who owned 500 - 999 slaves?

8. How many counties had individuals who owned 1000 or more slaves?

9. How many people were enslaved in slave counties?	10. How many people were enslaved in free counties?

11. Describe how slave states are similar. Describe how they are different.

Similar	Different

12. Why is it important to know the percentage of slaves in a county? How might counties with a low percentage of slaves be different than counties with a high percentage of slaves?

Name: _____ Date: _____ Class: _____

Economics by County – Student Answer Sheet

Directions: Use the ArcGIS Online map titled The 1860 Census: The Worlds of North and South to answer the following questions.

1. What patterns do you notice about manufacturing production at the county level in 1860?

Observations	Questions

2. What were the top four manufacturing counties in 1860? List them as County, State.

.

3. What was the total value of manufactured goods produced in slave counties?	4. What was the total value of manufactured goods produced in free counties?

5. What patterns do you notice about labor costs at the county level in 1860?

Observations	Questions

6. Which four counties had the highest labor costs in 1860? List them as County, State.

7. What were the total labor costs in slave counties?	8. What were the total labor costs in free counties?

9. Describe the differences in labor costs between free and slave counties.

10. How might this disparity affect the economies in the North and South?

Name: _____ Date: _____ Class: _____

Economic Detail by County – Student Answer Sheet

Directions: Use the ArcGIS Online map titled The 1860 Census: The Worlds of North and South to answer the following questions.

1. What patterns do you notice about cotton value at the county level in 1860?

Observations	Questions

2. What four counties had the highest cotton value in 1860? List them as County, State.

3. What was the total value of cotton in slave counties?	4. What was the total value of cotton in free counties?

5. What patterns do you notice about agricultural value at the county level in 1860?

Observations	Questions

6. Which four counties had the highest agricultural value in 1860? List them as County, State.

7. What was the total agricultural value in slave counties?	8. What was the total agricultural value in free counties?

9. **What patterns do you notice about access to railroads at the county level in 1860?**

Observations	Questions

10. How many counties had access to a railroad in slave states in 1860?	11. How many counties had access to a railroad in Free states in 1860?

Mapping U.S. History with GIS

134

Population and Slavery Answer Key

1. What patterns do you notice about the population distribution 1860? Record your observations and questions. **Northern states were more populated. Answers will vary.**
2. Which four states had the highest total population in 1860**? New York, Pennsylvania, Ohio, Illinois**
3. Which four states had the lowest total population in 1860? **Delaware, Florida, Minnesota, Rhode Island**
4. In 1860, how many states were Free States? **17**
5. In 1860, how many states were Slave States? **15**
6. What patterns do you notice about the slave population distribution in 1860? **Record your observations and questions. Virginia and the Deep South have a large number of slaves.**
7. Which four states had the highest slave population in 1860? **Virginia: 490,865; Georgia: 462,198; Mississippi: 436,631; Alabama: 435,080**
8. Which four states had the highest percentage of its population comprised of slaves in 1860? **South Carolina: 57%; Mississippi: 55%; Louisiana: 47%; Alabama: 45%**
9. Why do you think it is important to understand both the total number of slaves and percentage of slaves? Why might looking at just the total number of slaves be misleading? **In some states more than half the people living in the state were slaves.**
10. What do you notice about the distribution of major cities (those with more than 20,000 people)? Record your observations and questions. **Most are located in the North.**
11. How many major cities were located in slave states? **9**
12. How many major cities were located in Free states? **35**

Slavery by County Answer Key

1. What patterns do you notice about the distribution of slavery at the county level in 1860? **The counties with the highest slave percentages are located near the Mississippi River. Answers will vary.**
2. How many counties in the United States had population that was comprised of more the 50% slaves? **219 counties**
3. How many counties' population was comprised of more than 70% slaves? **52 counties**
4. How many counties' population was comprised of more than 90% slaves? **4 counties**
5. How many counties had individuals who owned 1 or more slaves? **1,088 counties**
6. How many counties had individuals who owned 50 – 99 slaves? **635 counties**
7. How many counties had individuals who owned 500 - 999 slaves? **10 counties**
8. How many counties had individuals who owned 1000 or more slaves? **1 county**
9. How many people were enslaved in slave counties? **3,950,511 people**
10. How many people were enslaved in free counties? **3,229 people**
11. Describe how slave states are similar. Describe how they are different. **Answers will vary**
12. Why is it important to know the percentage of slaves in a county? How might counties with a low percentage of slaves be different than counties with a high percentage of slaves? **Answers will vary. Counties with a high percentage of slaves will have very different needs and wants than a county with a low number of slaves.**

Economics by County Answer Key

1. What patterns do you notice about manufacturing production at the county level in 1860? **Most counties have very little manufacturing production. It is heavily concentrated in the Northeast.**
2. What were the top four manufacturing counties in 1860? **New York, NY; Philadelphia, PA; Hamilton, OH; Middlesex, MA**
3. What was the total value of manufactured goods produced in slave counties? **$ 286,876,240**
4. What was the total value of manufactured goods produced in free counties? **$ 1,573,906,515**
5. What patterns do you notice about labor costs at the county level in 1860? **Labor costs are considerably higher in the Northeast.**
6. Which four counties had the highest labor costs in 1860? New **York, NY; Philadelphia, PA; Essex, MA; Middlesex, MA**
7. What were the total labor costs in slave counties? **$ 50,266,547**
8. What were the total costs in free counties? **$ 309,704,570**
9. Describe the differences in labor costs between free and slave counties. **Labor costs in free counties much higher.**
10. How might this disparity affect the economies in the North and South? **The South can charge less for its goods. If it had to pay its slaves, its economy would take a hit.**

Economic Detail by County Answer Key

1. What patterns do you notice about cotton value at the county level in 1860? **Most of the counties are located in the South. Counties along the Mississippi River have the highest cotton value.**
2. What four counties had the highest cotton value in 1860? **Tensas, LA; Carroll, LA; Lawrence, TN, Yazoo,**
3. What was the total value of cotton in slave counties? **$ 258,591,440**
4. What was the total value of cotton in free counties? **$ 93,848**
5. What patterns do you notice about agricultural value at the county level in 1860? **Agricultural value is spread out. The North has fairly concentrated areas of high agricultural value.**
6. Which four counties had the highest agricultural value in 1860? **Lancaster, PA; Tensas, LA; St. Lawrence, NY; Chester, PA**
7. What was the total agricultural value in slave counties? **$ 796,192,486**
8. What was the total agricultural value in free counties? **$ 852,903,577**
9. What patterns do you notice about access to railroads at the county level in 1860? **Northern counties had much wider access to railroads.**
10. How many counties had access to a railroad in slave states in 1860? **297 counties**
11. How many counties had access to a railroad in Free states in 1860? **445 counties**

Chapter 7
Mapping the Civil War 1861-1865

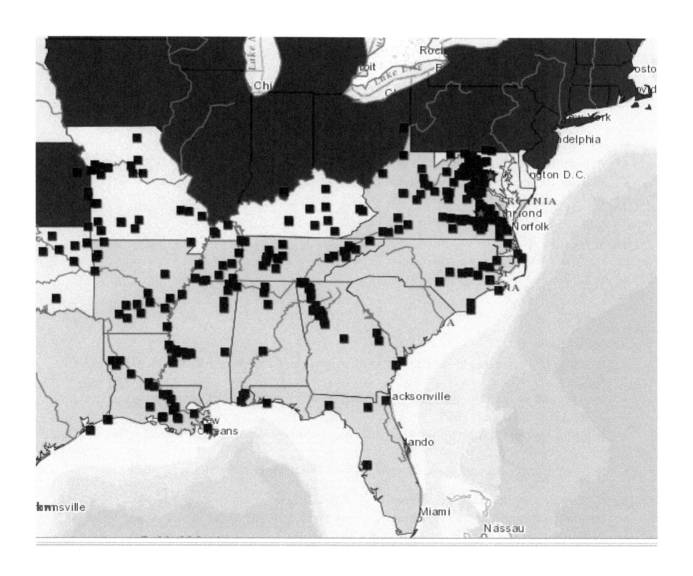

Mapping the Civil War: 1861-1865

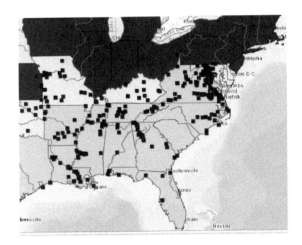

Introduction

This GIS investigation uses ArcGIS Online to explore the chronology of the major Civil War battles between 1861 and 1865. Divided into four activities this module has students identify geographic patterns, examine specific battle data, and analyze primary sources that relate to the Civil War.

Teacher Information

Time
- Activity One – Secession – 30-45 minutes
- Activity Two – The War Begins – 30-45 Minutes
- Activity Three – Anaconda Plan – 30-45 Minutes
- Activity Four – Total War – 30-45 Minutes

Subjects
United States History

Level
Grades 5-12

Objectives
Students will be able to:
- Identify the first states to secede and explain why the Confederate States seceded from the Union.
- Identify and explain the geographic distribution of major Civil Battles during the years of 1861, 1862, 1863, 1864, and 1865.
- Explain how the location of battles changed over time and provide a few explanations for the changes observed.
- Analyze primary sources to explain the context in which these battles took place.

Spatial Thinking Fundamentals/Themes
- Location – location of Civil War battles during 1861, 1862, 1863, 1864, and 1865.
- Region – Confederacy; Union; Mississippi River Valley
- Patterns – location of Civil War battles; where did they occur? Where did they not occur? Do you notice any concentrations?
- Comparison – comparing the location of battles during each year of the Civil War

Extensions

We recommend that you take advantage of ArcGIS Online's map notes functionality and assign groups of students one year of the war and task them with identifying and researching specific battles or strategies that occurred during that year. They should then plot some of these key events into map notes and present to their classmates. In the end you will have a great crowd-sourced map to share with parents, fellow teachers, and students. Once the map has been completed, students can also decide which battles and/or strategies were the most important within that year and in the larger picture of the war itself.

Students can also look through the Brady-Handy Collection from the Library of Congress (http://www.loc.gov/pictures/collection/brhc/) for that would help tell the story of some of the battles they've studied. Map notes can be created with links to pictures that will help other people understand the impact of the Civil War.

Mapping the Civil War: Secession - Instructions

Part I: A Country Divided

1. Go to http://gisetc.com/mushago. Open the map, **American Civil War**. Click **Modify Map**.
2. In front of you is a map of North America during the American Civil War.
3. **Click** the **Show Contents of Map** button so that all of the layers of the map become visible.
4. **Click** on **Civil War States** and **click** on **Show Legend icon**. Use the information to **answer question #1**.

> **Q1.**   What are the three categories that the states are grouped?

5. Click on each of the two capital cities on the map and **answer question #2**.

> **Q2.**   What are the names of the two capital cities during the Civil War?

Part II: Slave States and Free States

Let's find out how many states in 1861 allowed Slavery.

6. Hover over the layer named **Civil War States, click** on the layer and then **click** on the **Filter icon**.
7. Inside the **Filter** window create a filter that will display features in the **Civil War States** layer that match the expression **SLAVERY is YES.**
8. Choose **Apply Filter**

9. Show the table of filtered results by clicking the **Show Table icon below** the layer **Civil War States**.

10. Use the table to **answer questions #3, #4, and #5.**

> **Q3.**   How many states allowed slavery in 1861?
> **Q4.**   Which slave state's population had the highest percentage of slaves in 1861? What was the percentage? (HINT - sort PCTSLAVES to display descending)
> **Q5.**   Which slave state's population had the lowest percentage of slaves in 1861? What was the percentage? (HINT – sort PCTSLAVES to display ascending)

Part III: The South Secedes

Abraham Lincoln was elected President of the United States on November 6, 1860. His inauguration was held on March 4, 1861. Let's find out how many states seceded from the Union between the election and his inauguration.

11. Re-open the "Civil War States" **Filter** window by **clicking** on the **Filter icon**.
12. Inside the **Filter** window add a new expression to create a filter that will display features in the **Civil War States** layer whose **SECED_DATE is before 03/04/1861.**
13. Choose **Apply Filter.**

14. Show the table of filtered results by clicking the **Show Table icon** below the layer **Civil War States**.
15. Find out which state seceded first by **sorting** the table based on **SECED_DATE** in **ascending order**. (HINT – click on the field titled SECED_DATE and choose Sort Ascending.)
16. Use the filter results to **answer question - # 6 - #8** on your answer sheet.

     Q6.   **How many states seceded from the Union after Lincoln's election and before his inauguration on March 4, 1861?**

     Q7.   **Which state seceded first?**

     Q8.   **Look at the map describing the first states that chose to secede. Describe where these states were located.**

17. Next find out which states seceded after Lincoln's inauguration (03/04/1861). Re-open the **Civil War States Filter** window the same way you did in step 11.

18. Inside the **Filter** window change the current expression to create a filter that will display features in the Civil War States layer, **SECED_DATE is after 03/04/1861.**

19. Choose **Apply Filter.**
20. Show the table of filtered results by **clicking** the **Show Table icon** below the layer **Civil War States.**
21. Use this table and the map to **answer questions #9 - #12.**

     Q9.   **How many states seceded after Lincoln's inauguration?**

     Q10.   **Which state was the first to secede after his inauguration? What was the date?**

     Q11.   **Look at the map describing this second "wave" of secession. Describe where were these states were located. How is their location different from the first wave of secession?**

     Q12.   **How many slave states did not secede from the Union? What was the name given to these states? (HINT – Look in the legend)**

22. Re-open the Civil War States **Filter** window and click on **Remove Filter.**

Part IV: Primary Focus
23. **Turn on ☑ the Primary Sources layer.**
24. Click on the map note located in the middle of South Carolina titled **The Secession Begins.** Follow the link inside this map note to the Library of Congress' webpage. **Use this primary source to answer questions 13 through 15 on the answer worksheet.**

Mapping the Civil War: The War Begins - Instructions

Part I: 1861 Battles

1. Go to http://gisetc.com/mushago. Open the map, **American Civil War**. Click **Modify Map**.
2. In front of you is a map of North America during the America Civil War. Use the map and the map key to answer question 1 on "The War Begins" answer sheet.
3. Turn on ☑ the layer, 1861 Battles. Look at the location of 1861 battles to **answer question #1.**

> **Q1.** What patterns do you observe about the location of the early battles of the Civil War? What are some possible explanations for this pattern?

4. Show the table for 1861 battles by clicking on the **Show Table icon** to find out which of the early battles had the highest number of casualties.

5. **Sort** the table by **TotCas** (Total Casualties) in **descending order. Answer questions #2 - #4.**

> **Q2.** How many battles occurred in 1861?
> **Q3.** What was the casualty count in 1861? (HINT – Choose Statistics for TotCas)
> **Q4.** Which two battles experienced the highest number of casualties in 1861? (HINT – Choose Sort Descending for TotCas)

Washington, DC, Richmond, VA and the Mississippi River were important to both sides of the Civil War. Let's see what role these two factors played in the 1861 battles.

6. Hover over and click on the layer **1861 Battles. Click** on the **Filter icon.**
7. Inside the Filter window build an expression that will display all 1861 battles that occurred within 50 miles of a capital city (NEAR_CAP). The expression should read **NEAR_CAP is YES.**

8. Choose **Apply Filter.**

9. Show the table of filtered results by clicking the **Show Table icon** below the layer **1861 Battles.** Use this table to **answer question #5** on the answer sheet.

> **Q5.** In 1861, how many battles occurred within 50 miles of Richmond or Washington, DC?

Next, let's find out how many battles occurred within 25 miles of river that is part of the Mississippi River system.

10. Re-open the **1861 Battles Filter** window by clicking on the **Filter icon.**
11. Inside the **Filter** window **change the last expression** to create an expression that will display all 1861 battles that occurred within 25 miles of the Mississippi River System. The expression should read **NEAR_MISS is YES.**
12. Choose **Apply Filter**.
13. Show the table of filtered results by clicking the **Show Table icon** below the layer **1861 Battles.** Use this table to **answer question #6** on the answer sheet.

> **Q6.** In 1861, how many battles occurred within 25 miles of the Mississippi River System?

Now, let's find out where Robert E. Lee and Ulysses S. Grant were fighting in 1861.

14. Re-open the 1861 Battle" **Filter** window by clicking on the **Filter icon**. **Click** on **Remove Filter**
15. Inside the **Filter** window add a new expression to create a filter that will display features in the 1861 layer that meet **ANY** of the following expressions:
    CSACom contains Lee
    USACom contains Grant

16. Choose **Apply Filter.**
17. Show the table of filtered results by clicking the **Show Table icon** below the layer **1861 Battles**. Use the map and the table to **answer question #7.**

    Q7. **Where did Generals Robert E. Lee and Ulysses S. Grant fight in 1861?**

Part II: Primary Focus
18. Turn on the Primary Sources layer.
19. Click on the map note located in Virginia titled "Bull Run". Follow the link inside this map note to the Library of Congress' webpage. Be sure to click on the **View Transcription** link. Use this primary source to **answer questions #8 - #11** on the answer worksheet.

    Q8. **Who won the Battle of Bull Run (Manassas)?**
    Q9. **Why was this significant?**
    Q10. **Why does John Nicolay, Lincoln's secretary, say, "Our worst fears are confirmed?"**
    Q11. **Based on this letter, what can you infer about how the Union believed the battle would go?**

Mapping the Civil War: Anaconda Plan - Instructions

Part I: 1862 Battles

1. Go to http://gisetc.com/mushago. Open the map, **American Civil War**. Click **Modify Map**.
2. Turn on the 1862 Battles layer. Use this map to **answer question #1** on your answer sheet.

   Q1. **What are some of the patterns you notice with regards to the location of Civil War battles in 1862? What are some possible explanations?**

Next, let's find out how many battles occurred in 1862 by using the Filter command.

3. Hover over and click on the layer named **1862 Battle**. Click on the **Filter icon**.
4. Inside the **Filter** window create a filter that will display features in the Civil War States layer that match the expression **BEGIN_YEAR is 1862.**
5. Choose **Apply Filter.**
6. Show the table of filtered results by clicking the **Show Table icon** below the **1862 Battles layer.** Use this table to **answer questions #2, #3, and #4.**

   Q2. **How many battles occurred in 1862?**
   Q3. **What was the casualty count in 1862? (HINT – Choose Statistics for TotCas)**
   Q4. **Which three battles experienced the highest number of casualties in 1862?**

Washington, DC, Richmond, VA and the Mississippi River were important to both sides of the Civil War. Let's see what role these two factors played in the 1862 battles.

7. Re-open the **1862 Battles Filter** window by clicking on the **Filter icon.**
8. Inside the **Filter** window **add a new expression** to the existing filter. Build an expression that will display all 1862 battles that occurred within 50 miles of a capital city (NEAR_CAP). The expression should read **NEAR_CAP is YES.**
9. Choose **Apply Filter.**
10. Show the table of filtered results by clicking the **Show Table icon** below the **1862 Battles layer.** Use this table to **answer question #5** on the answer sheet.

    Q5. **In 1862, how many battles occurred within 50 miles of Richmond or Washington, DC?**

Next, let's find out how many battles occurred within 25 miles of a river that is part of the Mississippi River system.

11. Re-open the "1862 Battles" **Filter** window by clicking the **Filter icon.**
12. Inside the **Filter window** change the last expression to create an expression that will display all 1862 battles that occurred within 25 miles of the Mississippi River System. The expression should read **NEAR_MISS is YES.**
13. Choose **Apply Filter.**
14. Show the table of filtered results by clicking the **Show Table** icon below the 1862 Battles layer. Use this table to **answer question #6** on the answer sheet.

    Q6. **In 1862, how many battles occurred within 25 miles of the Mississippi River System?**

Now, let's find out where Robert E. Lee and Ulysses S. Grant were fighting in 1862.

15. Re-open the "1862 Battles" **Filter** window and click on **Remove Filter**.
16. Inside the **Filter** window add a new expression to create a filter that will display features in the 1862 layer that meet **ANY** of the following expressions:

    CSACom contains Lee
    USACom contains Grant

17. Choose **Apply Filter**
18. Show the table of filtered results by clicking the **Show Table icon** below the **1862 Battles layer**. Use the map and the table to **answer question #7**.

    Q7. **Where did Generals Robert E. Lee and Ulysses S. Grant fight in 1862?**

Part II: 1863 Battles

19. Turn on the 1863 Battles layer. Use this map to **answer question #8** on your answer sheet.

    Q8. **What are some of the patterns you notice with regards to the location of Civil War battles in 1863? Are there any similarities and/or differences when compared to the battles of 1862?**

Next, find out the same information for 1863 battles that you found out earlier for 1862 battles. Use the **1863 Battles layer** and the **Filter** and **Show Table** functions to **answer questions #9 - #14**.

    Q9. **How many battles occurred in 1863?**
    Q10. **What was the casualty count in 1863? (HINT – Choose Statistics for TotCas)**
    Q11. **Which three battles experienced the highest number of casualties in 1863?**
    Q12. **In 1863, how many battles occurred within 50 miles of Richmond or Washington, DC?**
    Q13. **In 1863, how many battles occurred within 25 miles of the Mississippi River System?**
    Q14. **Where did Generals Robert E. Lee and Ulysses S. Grant fight in 1863?**

Part III: Primary Focus

20. Turn on the Primary Sources layer.
21. **Click** on the map note located in the Gulf of Mexico titled, **The Anaconda Plan**. Follow the link inside this map note to the Library of Congress' webpage. Use this primary source to **answer questions #15 - #17** on the answer worksheet.

    Q15. **Describe what the snake is doing in this picture.**
    Q16. **How does the Civil War battle map from 1862-1863 look similar to the cartoon?**
    Q17. **How is it different?**

Mapping the Civil War: Total War - Instructions

Part I: *1864 Battles*

1. Go to http://gisetc.com/mushago. Open the map, **American Civil War**. Click **Modify Map**.
2. Turn on the **1864 Battles** layer. Use this map to **answer question #1** on your answer sheet.

> **Q1.** What are some of the patterns you notice with regards to the location of Civil War battles in 1864? How does this year's battle locations compare to the previous three years of battles (1861, 1862, 1863)?

Next, let's find out how many battles occurred in 1864 by using the **Filter** command.

3. Hover over and click on the **1864 Battles** layer. **Click** on the **Filter icon.**
4. Inside the **Filter** window create a filter that will display features in the Civil War States layer that match the expression **BEGIN_YEAR is 1864.**
5. Choose **Apply Filter.**
6. Show the table of filtered results by clicking the **Show Table icon** below the **1864 Battles layer.** Use this table to **answer questions #2, #3, and #4.**

> **Q2.** How many battles occurred in 1864?
> **Q3.** What was the casualty count in 1864? (HINT – Choose Statistics for TotCas)
> **Q4.** Which three battles experienced the highest number of casualties in 1864?

Washington, DC, Richmond, VA and the Mississippi River were important to both sides of the Civil War. Let's see what role these two factors played in the 1864 battles.

7. Re-open the "1864 Battles" **Filter window** by **clicking** on the **Filter icon.**
8. Inside the **Filter** window add a new expression to the existing filter. Now build an expression that will display all 1864 battles that occurred within 50 miles of a capital city (NEAR_CAP). The expression should read **NEAR_CAP is YES.**

9. Choose **Apply Filter.**

10. Show the table of filtered results by clicking the **Show Table icon** below the **1864 Battles layer.** Use this table to **answer question #5** on the answer sheet.

> **Q5.** In 1864, how many battles occurred within 50 miles of Richmond or Washington, DC?

Next, let's find out how many battles occurred within 25 miles of a river that is part of the Mississippi River system.

11. Re-open the **1864 Battles Filter** window by **clicking** on the **Filter icon.**
12. Inside the **Filter change the last expression** to create an expression that will display all 1864 battles that occurred within 25 miles of the Mississippi River System. The expression should read **NEAR_MISS is YES.**
13. Choose **Apply Filter.**
14. Show the table of filtered results by clicking the **Show Table icon** below the **1864 Battles layer.** Use this table to **answer question #6** on the answer sheet.

> **Q6.** In 1864, how many battles occurred within 25 miles of the Mississippi River System?

Now, let's find out where Robert E. Lee and Ulysses S. Grant were fighting in 1864.

15. **Re-open** the 1864 Battles **Filter** window by **clicking** on the **Filter icon. Remove all Filter.**

16. Inside the **Filter** window add a new expression to create a filter that will display features in the 1864 layer that meet **ANY** of the following expressions:

    CSACom contains Lee
    USACom contains Grant

17. Choose **Apply Filter**

18. Show the table of filtered results by clicking the **Show Table** icon below the 1864 Battles layer. Use the map and the table to **answer question #7.**

    Q7.   Where did Generals Robert E. Lee and Ulysses S. Grant fight in 1864?

19. **Create a filter to find out where William T. Sherman fought in 1864. Use the results of this filter to answer question #8. (HINT – Filter for USACom contains Sherman)**

    Q8.   Where did General William T. Sherman fight battles in 1864? Do you notice a pattern for the locations of these battles?

Part II: 1865 Battles

20. Turn on the 1865 Battles layer.   Use this map to **answer question #9** on your answer sheet.

    Q9.   What are some of the patterns you notice with regards to the location of Civil War battles in 1865? How does this year's battles compare to the battles of the last four years?

21. Next, find out the same information for 1865 battles that you have found out for 1861, 1862, 1863, and 1864 battles. Use the 1865 Battles layer and the **Filter** and **Show Table** functions to answer questions #10 through #15.

    Q10.   How many battles occurred in 1865?
    Q11.   What was the casualty count in 1865? (HINT – Choose Statistics for TotCas)
    Q12.   Which three battles experienced the highest number of casualties in 1865?
    Q13.   In 1865, how many battles occurred within 50 miles of Richmond or Washington, DC?
    Q14.   In 1865, how many battles occurred within 25 miles of the Mississippi River System?
    Q15.   Where did Generals Robert E. Lee and Ulysses S. Grant fight in 1865?

Part III: Primary Focus

22. Turn on the **Primary Sources** layer.

23. Click on the map note located in Georgia, "March to the Sea." Follow the links inside this map note to the Library of Congress' webpage. Use these primary sources to **answer questions #16 and #17** on the answer worksheet.

    Q16.   Why are Sherman's men destroying the railroads?
    Q17.   Based on these pictures, how did total war affect the people living in the pathway of Sherman's March?

Name: _____ Date: _____ Class: _____

Secession – Student Answer Sheet

Directions: Use the ArcGIS Online map titled The Civil War: 1861-1865 to answer the following questions.

Map Analysis

1. Into which three categories are the states grouped?

2. What are the names of the two capital cities during the Civil War?

3. How many states allowed slavery in 1861?

4. Which slave state's population had the highest percentage of slaves? What was the percentage?

5. Which slave state's population had the lowest percentage of slaves in 1861? What was the percentage?

6. How many states seceded from the Union after Lincoln's election and before his inauguration on March 4, 1861?

7. Which state seceded first?

8. Look at the map describing the first states that seceded. Describe where these states were located.

9. How many states seceded after Lincoln's inauguration?

10. Which state was the first to secede after his inauguration? What was the date?

11. Look at the map describing this second "wave" of secession. Describe where these states are located. How is their location different from the first wave of secession?

12. How many slave states did not secede from the Union? What were these states called?

Primary Source Analysis

13. Which states are represented in this cartoon?

14. Which eventual Confederate States of America members are missing?

15. Why aren't all of the states represented?

Name: _____ Date: _____ Class: _____

The War Begins – Student Answer Sheet

Directions: Use the ArcGIS Online map titled The Civil War: 1861-1865 to answer the following questions.

Map Analysis

1. What patterns do you observe about the location of the early battles of the Civil War? What are some possible explanations for this pattern?

Patterns	Explanations

2. How many battles occurred in 1861?

3. What was the casualty count in 1861?

4. Which two battles experienced the highest number of casualties in 1861?

5. In 1861, how many battles occurred within 50 miles of Richmond or Washington, DC?

6. In 1861, how many battles occurred within 25 miles of the Mississippi River System?

7. Where did Generals Robert E. Lee and Ulysses S. Grant fight in 1861?

Primary Source Analysis

8. Who won the Battle of Bull Run (Manassas)?

9. Why was this significant?

10. Why does John Nicolay, Lincoln's secretary, say, "Our worst fears are confirmed?"

11. Based on this letter, what can you infer about how the Union believed the battle would go?

Name: _____ Date: _____ Class: _____

Anaconda Plan – Student Answer Sheet

Directions: Use the ArcGIS Online map titled The Civil War: 1861-1865 to answer the following questions.

Map Analysis

1. What are some patterns you notice with regards to the location of Civil War battles in 1862? What are some possible explanations?

Patterns	Explanations

2. How many battles occurred in 1862?

3. Which battle had the highest number of casualties in 1862? How many casualties?

4. What was the casualty count in 1862?

5. In 1862, how many battles occurred within 50 miles of Richmond or Washington, D.C.?

6. In 1862, how many battles occurred within 25 miles of the Mississippi River System?

7. Where did Generals Robert E. Lee and Ulysses S. Grant fight in 1862?

8. What are some patterns you notice with regards to the location of the Civil War battles in 1863? Are there any similarities and/or differences when compared to the battles of 1862?

Patterns	Similarities	Differences

9. How many battles occurred in 1863?

10. What was the casualty count in 1863?

11. Which three battles experienced the highest number of casualties in 1863?

12. In 1863, how many battles occurred within 50 miles of Richmond or Washington, D.C.?

13. In 1863, how many battles occurred within 25 miles of the Mississippi River System?

14. Where did Generals Robert E. Lee and Ulysses S. Grant fight in 1863?

Primary Source Analysis

15. Describe what the snake is doing in this picture.

16. How does the Civil War battle map from 1862-1863 look similar to the cartoon?

17. How is it different?

Name: _____ Date: _____ Class: _____

Total War – Student Answer Sheet

Directions: Use the ArcGIS Online map titled The Civil War: 1861-1865 to answer the following questions.

Map Analysis

1. What are some of the patterns you notice with regards to the location of Civil War battles in 1864? How does this year's battle locations compare to the previous three years of battles?

Patterns	Comparisons

2. How many battles occurred in 1864?

3. What was the casualty count in 1864?

4. Which three battles experienced the highest number of casualties?

5. In 1864, how many battles occurred within 50 miles of Richmond or Washington, D.C.?

6. In 1864, how many battles occurred within 25 miles of the Mississippi River System?

7. Where did Generals Robert E. Lee and Ulysses S. Grant fight in 1864?

8. Where did General William T. Sherman fight battles in 1864? Do you notice a pattern for the locations of these battles?

9. What are some patterns you notice with regards to the location of the Civil War battles in 1865? How does this year's battles compare to the battles of the past four years?

Patterns	Similarities	Differences

10. How many battles occurred in 1865?

11. What was the casualty count in 1865?

12. Which three battles experienced the highest number of casualties in 1865?

13. In 1865, how many battles occurred within 50 miles of Richmond or Washington, D.C.?

14. In 1865, how many battles occurred within 25 miles of the Mississippi River System?

15. Where did Generals Robert E. Lee and Ulysses S. Grant fight in 1865?

Primary Source Analysis

16. Why are Sherman's men destroying the railroads?

17. Based on these pictures, how did total war affect the people living in the pathway of Sherman's March?

ArcGIS Online How-To

For folks that need a pictorial view of some functions of ArcGIS online that we used throughout the lessons, we've provided these steps. Keep in mind that ArcGIS online is updated often and the exact view may have changed since the latest printing of this text. We endeavor to keep it updated as the tools change. If you have questions, please feel free to email us, info@gisetc.com.

 CHANGING SYMBOLS (Changing Styles)

1. Make sure that Details and Content are selected.
2. **Click** on the **layer name** in the content list to see the options for that layer: legend, table, Change Style (Symbols), filter and more options.

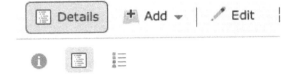

☑ United States 1790

3. **Click** the **Change Style icon** .

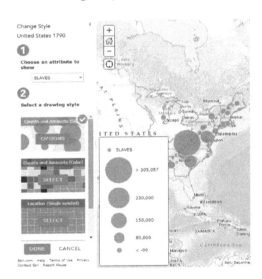 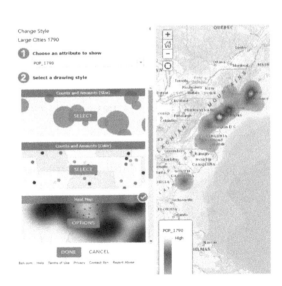

4. First, **select** the **attribute** (feature) of the data that you would like for the map to display. Your options vary based on the data.
5. Second, **select** from the **drawing style**. The display will preview the data for you on the map. The default style in AGO is single symbol (all items the same color).
   a. If you want a **thematic map**, you'll most likely need to **select counts and amounts (size) or counts and amounts (color).**
   b. If you want a **unique color for each individual item**, then **select location (unique symbol)**.
6. Click **OPTIONS** to change colors or size of symbols. Also this will allow you to aggregate the data, such as normalize based on population.

7. Click **OK** to save your options.
8. Click **DONE** to return to the Contents.

FILTERING FEATURES

Sometimes you will be asked to filter a layer's features so that the map only displays features that meet certain criteria. The steps below walk you through filtering the number of US States in 1861 that allowed slavery. To do this:

1. Make sure that **Details** and **Content** are selected.
2. **Click** on the **layer name** in the content list to see the options for that layer: legend, table, Change Style (Symbols), filter and more options.

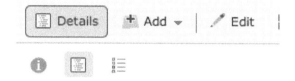

1. **Click** the **filter** icon .
2. Inside the Filter window create a filter that will display features, such as in the Civil War States layer that might filter the data with the expression "SLAVERY is YES."
   a. You have three options for filtering a data field. Most often you'll likely utilize VALUE and UNIQUE.
      i. Value (you type in the value)
      ii. Field (you select another field to compare with)
      iii. Unique (you select a value provided by the data field)

3. **Click Apply Filter**. Notice that only the items that match the expression are visible.
4. To **remove a filter, click** the **Filter** icon and **select Remove Filter**.

TABLES

Sometimes you will be asked to sort data from the table in ascending order (to find the lowest value of a field) or descending order (to find out the highest value in a field). Other times you will be asked to gather some statistics.

1. Make sure that **Details** and **Content** are selected.
2. **Click** on the **layer name** in the content list to see the options for that layer: legend, table, Change Style (Symbols), filter and more options.

☑ United States 1790

3. **Click** the **Table icon** below the layer name.
4. The Table containing the data for that layer will appear below the map.

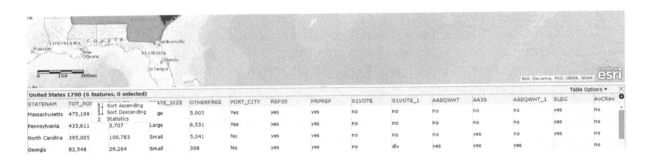

STATENAM	TOT_POP			TE_SIZE	OTHERFREE	PORT_CITY	REP35	PRPREP	S1VOTE	S1VOTE_1	AAEQWHT	AA35	AAEQWHT_1	SLEG	AoCRev
Massachusetts	475,199	↓ Sort Ascending ↑ Sort Descending Σ Statistics		ge	5,905	Yes	yes	yes	no	no	no	no	no	yes	no
Pennsylvania	433,611	3,707		Large	6,531	Yes	yes	yes	no	no	no	no	no	yes	no
North Carolina	395,005	100,783		Small	5,041	No	yes	yes	no	no	no	yes	no	yes	no
Georgia	82,548	29,264		Small	398	No	yes	yes	no	div	yes	yes	yes		no

 STATISTICS

1. To find out the total population of the United States, click the top of the data field so that the small window appears with two sort choices and Statistics.
2. Choose Statistics to get summative information on that data field.
3. Click close or the X in the corner to hide the window.

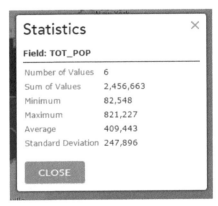

Statistics ✕

Field: **TOT_POP**

Number of Values	6
Sum of Values	2,456,663
Minimum	82,548
Maximum	821,227
Average	409,443
Standard Deviation	247,896

CLOSE

SORTING ASCENDING OR DESCENDING

1. Click on the top of the data field so the small window appears with two sort choices and statistics.
2. Choose the sort you want ascending (A to Z for text; small to large for numbers) or descending (Z to A for text; large to small for numbers).
3. The data table will sort for you on the fly.

 DRAWING GRAPHICS

Sometimes you may need to draw graphics on the map. To draw on the map follow the steps below. You may need to be signed into ArcGIS Online to use this feature.

1. Create a Map Notes Layer to add points, lines, or areas to a map. Go to Add -> Add Map Notes

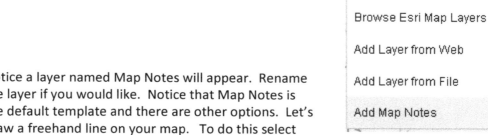

2. Notice a layer named Map Notes will appear. Rename the layer if you would like. Notice that Map Notes is the default template and there are other options. Let's draw a freehand line on your map. To do this select the "Freehand Line" feature to add.

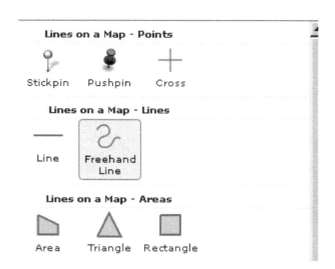

3. Click and hold and then draw a freehand line anywhere on your map. Notice that a description window appears. Inside this window you can add a description, a hyperlink, and choose to change the color or symbol for the feature you have drawn.

Editing the Graphics Drawing

Once you create features you can edit them. To edit a feature you have added to the map follow these steps.

1. With Details format active hover over and select any feature that you have created. Notice the information window for that feature will appear.
2. At the bottom of this window is an option to edit the feature. Choose Edit.

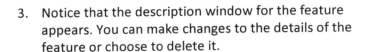

3. Notice that the description window for the feature appears. You can make changes to the details of the feature or choose to delete it.

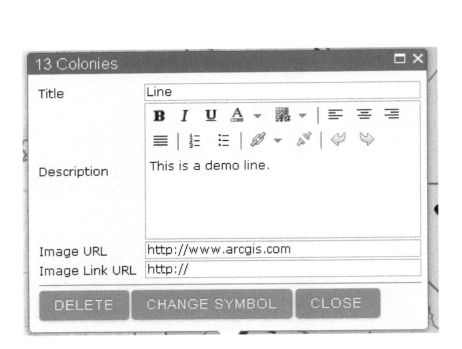

Resources

Inter-University Consortium for Political and Social Research. Historical, Demographic, Economic, and Social Data: The United States, 1790 – 2002. (ICPSR 2896). Ann Arbor, Michigan.

Great Roads of Colonial America - http://www.genealogyblog.com/?p=19649

Fall Line Road - http://www.carolana.com/NC/Royal_Colony/the_fall_line_road.html

Early American Roads and Trails, *Beverly Whitaker, Kansas City, Missouri, Copyright 2002. Online <http://freepages.genealogy.rootsweb.com/~gentutor/trails.html>*

Credits and Sources
Credits are listed by topic.

Jamestown (London to the Fall Line)
Virginia Shapefiles:
These files contain state and county boundary information for Virginia: VA_1890, VA_1860, VA_1790, VA_1780, VA_1750, VA_1700, and VA_1634.

Courtesy of: *Virginia Atlas of Historical County Boundaries*
Long, John H., Editor; Peggy Tuck Sinko, Historical Compiler; Gordon Den Boer, Historical Compiler; Laura Rico-Beck, GIS Specialist and Digital Compiler; Peter Siczewicz, ArcIMS Interactive Map Designer; Emily Kelley, Research Associate; Robert Will, Cartographic Assistant; Copyright: The Newberry Library, 2003

Virginia Census Variables:
These files contain census data for Virginia from the years 1790, 1860, and 1890.
VA_1890, VA_1860, VA_1790, VA_1780, VA_1750, VA_1700, VA_1634
Courtesy of: *Historical, Demographic, Economic, and Social Data: The United States, 1790 – 2002. (ICPSR 2896).*
Inter-University Consortium for Political and Social Research. Ann Arbor, Michigan.

Jamestowne Voyage Place marks:
This file contains place marks for a selection of stops made during the Virginia Company's 1607 voyage to Jamestown.
Created by Chris Bunin. Dates courtesy of the Jamestown Settlement Museum. "Significant Events in Jamestown History". *Jamestown Settlement and Yorktown Victory Center.* 31 Dec 2013.
http://historyisfun.org/Jamestown-Chrono.htm

John Smith's Account:
This contains primary source information about the voyage to Jamestown, detailed by John Smith in 1612.
Smith, John. "The Proceedings and Accidents of the English Colony in Virginia." 1612. TS. Library of Congress, Washington, D.C. *Library of Congress Website.* 31 Dec 2013
http://www.loc.gov/teachers/classroommaterials/presentationsandactivities/presentations/timeline/colonial/jamestwn/colonist.html

Why Yorktown?
Major Battles:
This file contains information about the major battles fought during the American Revolution.
This file was compiled and created by Donna Shifflett and Chris Bunin as part of *The Virginia Experiment*, a Teaching American History grant. 2007. Courtesy of Albemarle County Schools, Charlottesville City Schools, Greene County Schools, Madison County Schools and Orange County Schools.

Data is courtesy of the National Park Service. *The Revolutionary War & War of 1812 Historic Preservation Study*, http://www.nps.gov/history/hps/abpp/rev1812.htm, December 8, 2007

Original 13 States Shapefiles:
This file contains state boundaries for the original 13 states.
This shapefile was downloaded from http://www.nhgis.org and is provided courtesy of the National Historical GIS. Minnesota Population Center. *National Historical Geographic Information System: Version 2.0*. Minneapolis, MN: University of Minnesota 2011.

Original 13 States 1790 Census Variables:
This file contains state-level 1790 census data.
Data courtesy of the Inter-University Consortium of Political and Social Research.
Historical, Demographic, Economic, and Social Data: The United States, 1790 – 2002. (ICPSR 2896). Inter-University Consortium for Political and Social Research. Ann Arbor, Michigan.

Major Cities:
This file contains location information for the largest 100 cities as listed in the 1790 census.
This file was compiled by Chris Bunin. Data courtesy of the U.S. Census Bureau.
Gibson, Campbell. *Population of the 100 Largest Cities and Other Urban Places in the United States: 1790 to 1990.* U. S. Census Bureau. N.d. Web. Accessed: 2007.
<http://www.census.gov/population/www/documentation/twps0027/twps0027.html>

Southern Campaign:
This file contains information the battles fought during the American Revolution as part of Nathanael Greene's campaign.
This file was compiled by Donna Shifflett and Chris Bunin as part of *The Virginia Experiment*, a Teaching American History grant. 2007. Courtesy of Albemarle County Schools, Charlottesville City Schools, Greene County Schools, Madison County Schools and Orange County Schools.

Primary Source:
Illman Brothers. *The Surrender of Cornwallis at Yorktown.* 1870. Library of Congress. Web. 31 Dec 2013.
<http://lcweb2.loc.gov/service/pnp/pga/01600/01668v.jpg>

Major Rivers
This file contains data on the major river systems in the United States.
Data courtesy of ESRI, Redlands, California

Major Lakes:
This file contains data on the major lakes in the United States.
Data courtesy of ESRI, Redlands, California

Southern Campaign Locations
These files contain some of the key locations of General Greene's Southern Campaign during the American Revolution: Crossing the Dan, Cowpens, Cowan's Ford, Haw River, Guilford Court House, Augusta, Hobkirk's Hill, Camden, Ninety-Six, and Eutaw Springs
Each of these point files were compiled and created by Chris Bunin.

Constitutional Convention
United States, 1790 Shapefile:
This file contains the 1790 boundaries of each state in the United States. This shapefile was downloaded from http://www.nhgis.org and is provided courtesy of the National Historical GIS. Minnesota Population Center. *National Historical Geographic Information System: Version 2.0*. Minneapolis, MN: University of Minnesota 2011.

United States, 1790 Census Variables:
This file contains data from the 1790 Census pertaining to the population and slave totals in each state.
Data courtesy of the Inter-University Consortium of Political and Social Research.
Historical, Demographic, Economic, and Social Data: The United States, 1790 – 2002. (ICPSR 2896). Inter-University Consortium for Political and Social Research. Ann Arbor, Michigan.

United States, 1790 Constitutional Convention Vote Data:
This file contains vote data from the Constitutional Convention held from 1787. The following votes are included in this file:

- PRPREP: Should states be represented proportionally in Congress?
- S1VOTE: Should states have equal representation in the Senate?
- AAEQWHT: Should African-Americans be counted equal to whites?
- AA35: Should African-Americans be counted as 3/5 of a person?
- AoCREV: Should we revise the Articles of Confederation?
- NJVA: Should we proceed with the Virginia Plan?

The vote data was compiled by Christine Esposito using James Madison's notes from the Constitutional Convention as part of *The Virginia Experiment*, a Teaching American History grant. 2007. Courtesy of Albemarle County Schools, Charlottesville City Schools, Greene County Schools, Madison County Schools and Orange County Schools.

Madison, James. *Notes of Debates in the Federal Convention of 1787.* New York: W. Norton, 1987. Print.

Large Cities, 1790:
This file contains location and population data on the largest cities in the United States in 1790. This file was compiled by Chris Bunin. Data courtesy of the U.S. Census Bureau.
Gibson, Campbell. *Population of the 100 Largest Cities and Other Urban Places in the United States: 1790 to 1990.* U. S. Census Bureau. N.d. Web. Accessed: 2007.
<http://www.census.gov/population/www/documentation/twps0027/twps0027.html>

Large Port Cities, 1790:
This file contains location and population data on port cities in the United States in 1790. It is a subset of the Large Cities, 1790 data set. This file was created by Christine Esposito, derived from data compiled by Chris Bunin. Data courtesy of the U.S. Census Bureau.
Gibson, Campbell. *Population of the 100 Largest Cities and Other Urban Places in the United States: 1790 to 1990.* U. S. Census Bureau. N.d. Web. Accessed: 2007.
<http://www.census.gov/population/www/documentation/twps0027/twps0027.html>

Major Rivers, 1790
This file contains data on the major river systems in the United States. It has been edited to include only those river systems which were a part of the United States in 1790.
Data courtesy of ESRI, Redlands, California

Territorial Expansion
Territory Shapefiles:
These shapefiles contain information on each of the territorial acquisitions made by the United States from 1803 to 1848: California, Florida, Gadsden, Oregon, Texas, Louisiana Purchase, United States, 1783.
Each shapefile of the acquired territories was derived from the National Atlas of the United States. Additional information on the area of each acquisition was found in the *New York Times* article cited below.
National Atlas of the United States, 200506, Territorial Acquisitions of the United States: National Atlas of the United States, Reston, VA. <http://nationalatlas.gov/atlasftp.html>
"Uncle Sam's Real Estate". *New York Times* 4 February 1912: Online. <http://query.nytimes.com/mem/archive-free/pdf?res=F70C11FB3C5813738DDDAD0894DA405B828DF1D3>

New Orleans: This file contains the location of the city of New Orleans. This file was created by Chris Bunin.

territorial_expansion - Lakes: This file contains data on the major lakes in the United States. Data courtesy of ESRI, Redlands, California

territorial_expansion - MajorRivers: This file contains data on the major river systems in the United States. Data courtesy of ESRI, Redlands, California

Primary Sources-
California:
"The Treaty of Guadalupe Hidalgo". *Library of Congress.* Hispanic Area Division Studies. February 14, 2011. Web. 31 Dec 2013. <http://www.loc.gov/rr/hispanic/ghtreaty/>
Florida:
"The Culture and History of the Americas: The Jay I. Kislak Collection at the Library of Congress". *Library of Congress.* N.d., July 27, 2010. Web. 31 Dec 2013 <http://www.loc.gov/exhibits/kislak/kislak-exhibit.html>
Texas:
"Today in History: Texas Annexation". *Library of Congress.* N.p., N.d. Web. 31 Dec 2013 <http://memory.loc.gov/ammem/today/jun23.html#annextexas>
Gadsden Purchase:
"Today in History: Gadsden Purchase." *Library of Congress.* N.p., N.d, Web. 31 Dec 2013. <http://memory.loc.gov/ammem/today/dec30.html>
Louisiana Purchase:
"Today in History: Westward Ho!" *Library of Congress.* N.p., N.d., Web. 31 Dec 2013. <http://memory.loc.gov/ammem/today/oct20.html>
Oregon Territory:
"Today in History: Oregon Territory." *Library of Congress.* N.p., N.d., Web. 31 Dec 2013 <http://memory.loc.gov/ammem/today/aug14.html>
US to 1800:
"Treaty of Paris". *Library of Congress.* N.p., N.d, Web. 31 Dec 2013. <http://www.ourdocuments.gov/doc.php?flash=true&doc=6>

Trails to Rails:
Major Cities:
These files contain the location and population of the largest cities, according to the US Census in 1790, 1810, 1830, and 1850: Major Cities, 1790, Major Cities, 1810, Major Cities, 1830, Major Cities, 1850.
These files were compiled by Chris Bunin. Data courtesy of the U.S. Census Bureau.
Gibson, Campbell. *Population of the 100 Largest Cities and Other Urban Places in the United States: 1790 to 1990.* U. S. Census Bureau. N.d. Web. Accessed: 2007.
<http://www.census.gov/population/www/documentation/twps0027/twps0027.html>

US States Shapefile:
This file contains the state boundaries in the current United States.
Files courtesy of ESRI, Redlands, California

Roads:
Early Roads - shows the colonial of roads of early America.
Shapefile created by Chris Bunin based on locations provided in *Early American Roads and Trails*, Beverly Whitaker, Kansas City, Missouri, Copyright 2002. Online http://freepages.genealogy.rootsweb.com/~gentutor/trails.html Accessed 2007.
The following files show the development of the National Road between 1818 – 1838. File researched and created by Chris Bunin: The National Road, 1818, The National Road, 1828, The National Road, 1838.

Major Canals, 1832 – shows the general extent of canal construction up until 1832. File researched and created by Chris Bunin

Sources consulted included:

- *Transportation Developments in the Early Republic*
  http://www.connerprairie.org/historyonline/travel.html Accessed January, 2008
- *The Steamboat Era*, A.W. Moore http://riverweb.cet.uiuc.edu/Archives/fwp/ Accessed January, 2008
- *Clinton's Big Ditch* http://www.eriecanal.org Accessed January, 2008
- *Transportation Revolution, 1815 – 1850*
  http://www.historicaltextarchive.com/sections.php?op=viewarticle&artid=646 Accessed January, 2008
- *Westward Expansion (1807-1912)* http://www.sparknotes.com/history/american/westwardexpansion/
  Accessed January, 2008
- *Wake Up, America* www.pbs.org/wnet/historyofus/web04/index.html Accessed 2007
- Stover, John F. *The Routledge Historical Atlas of the American Railroads*, Routledge Press. New York. 1999.

The following files show the general development of **major steamboat routes between 1810 and 1850**. Files researched and created by Chris Bunin: Major Steamboat Routes, 1810; Major Steamboat Routes, 1830; Major Steamboat Routes, 1850.
Sources consulted included:

- *Transportation Developments in the Early Republic*
  http://www.connerprairie.org/historyonline/travel.html Accessed January, 2008
- *The Steamboat Era*, A.W. Moore http://riverweb.cet.uiuc.edu/Archives/fwp/ Accessed January, 2008
- *Clinton's Big Ditch* http://www.eriecanal.org Accessed January, 2008
- *Transportation Revolution, 1815 – 1850*
  http://www.historicaltextarchive.com/sections.php?op=viewarticle&artid=646 Accessed January, 2008
- *Westward Expansion (1807-1912)* http://www.sparknotes.com/history/american/westwardexpansion/
  Accessed January, 2008
- *Wake Up, America* www.pbs.org/wnet/historyofus/web04/index.html Accessed 2007
- Stover, John F. *The Routledge Historical Atlas of the American Railroads*, Routledge Press. New York. 1999.

The following files show the development of **railroads between 1830 – 1850**: Railroads, 1830 and Railroads, 1850. Files courtesy of William G. Thomas, University of Nebraska.
Thomas, William G. *Railroads and the Making of Modern America: A Digital History Project.* University of Nebraska – Lincoln. http://railroads.unl.edu/ Accessed August, 2013.

Two Worlds

Large Cities:
This file contains the largest cities in the United States in 1860.
This file was compiled by Chris Bunin. Data courtesy of the U.S. Census Bureau.
Gibson, Campbell. *Population of the 100 Largest Cities and Other Urban Places in the United States: 1790 to 1990.*
U. S. Census Bureau. N.d. Web. Accessed: 2007.
<http://www.census.gov/population/www/documentation/twps0027/twps0027.html>

COUNTY_CENSUS_1860 Shapefile:
This file contains the county boundaries for the United States in 1860.
This shapefile was downloaded from http://www.nhgis.org and are provided courtesy of the National Historical GIS. Minnesota Population Center. *National Historical Geographic Information System: Version 2.0.* Minneapolis, MN: University of Minnesota 2011.

COUNTY_CENSUS_1860 Census Variables:
This file contains a variety of census data at the county level from the 1860 Census.
Data courtesy of the Inter-University Consortium of Political and Social Research.
Historical, Demographic, Economic, and Social Data: The United States, 1790 – 2002. (ICPSR 2896). Inter-University Consortium for Political and Social Research. Ann Arbor, Michigan.

STATE_CENSUS_1860 Shapefile:
This file contains the state boundaries for the United States in 1860. This shapefile was downloaded from http://www.nhgis.org and are provided courtesy of the National Historical GIS. Minnesota Population Center. *National Historical Geographic Information System: Version 2.0.* Minneapolis, MN: University of Minnesota 2011.

STATE_CENSUS_1860 Census Variables:
This file contains a variety of census data at the state level from the 1860 Census.
Data courtesy of the Inter-University Consortium of Political and Social Research.
Historical, Demographic, Economic, and Social Data: The United States, 1790 – 2002. (ICPSR 2896). Inter-University Consortium for Political and Social Research. Ann Arbor, Michigan.

Two_worlds_NorthSouth – Railroads – shows the extent of railroads in the United States in 1860.
Files courtesy of William G. Thomas, University of Nebraska.
Thomas, William G. *Railroads and the Making of Modern America: A Digital History Project.* University of Nebraska – Lincoln. http://railroads.unl.edu/ Accessed August, 2013.

Two_worlds_NorthSouth – MajorRivers – shows the major rivers in the United States.
Files courtesy of ESRI, Redlands, California

Civil War
Civil War Battles:
These files contain information on the major battles of the Civil War from 1861-1865: Civil_War – 1861, Civil_War – 1862, Civil_War – 1863, Civil_War – 1864, Civil_War – 1865, Civil_War - All Civil War Battles.
These files were compiled, based on data from the National Park Service, by Robert Stewart, Jeremy Newcomb, and Chris Bunin as part of *The Virginia Experiment*, a Teaching American History grant. 2007. Courtesy of Albemarle County Schools, Charlottesville City Schools, Greene County Schools, Madison County Schools and Orange County Schools.
Data courtesy of The National Park Service. "The Civil War, The American Battlefield Protection Program" http://www.nps.gov/history/hps/abpp/civil.htm, December 8, 2007, Accessed December, 2007

Civil War States:
This file contains the boundaries for each state in the United States in 1860.
This shapefile was created by dissolving ESRI's present-day US States shapefile.
Census variables courtesy of the Inter-University Consortium of Political and Social Research. Historical, *Demographic, Economic, and Social Data: The United States, 1790 – 2002. (ICPSR 2896).* Inter-University Consortium for Political and Social Research. Ann Arbor, Michigan.

Secession data compiled by Chris Bunin.
Civil_War - **Capital Cities** – shows the locations of Richmond and Washington, DC. Created by Chris Bunin
Civil_War - **Major_Rivers**: Data courtesy of ESRI, Redlands, California.

Primary Sources:
- John G. Nicolay (1832-1901) to Theresa Bates, July 21-22, 1861. John G. Nicolay Papers, Manuscript Division, Library of Congress. <http://www.loc.gov/exhibits/civil-war-in-america/ext/cw0032.html>
- Currier & Ives. *The Secession Movement.* c. 1861. Library of Congress. Web. 31 Dec 2013 < http://www.loc.gov/pictures/resource/cph.3a33510/>
- Elliot, J.B. *Scott's Great Snake.* 1861. Library of Congress. Web. 31 Dec 2013 < http://www.loc.gov/resource/g3701s.cw0011000/>
- Barnard, George. *On the Lines near Atlanta.* 1864. Library of Congress. Web. 31 Dec 2013 < http://www.loc.gov/pictures/resource/stereo.1s02539/>
- Taylor & Huntington. *How Sherman's Boys Fixed the Railroad.* 1864. Library of Congress. Web. 31 Dec 2013 < http://www.loc.gov/pictures/resource/stereo.1s02800/>

Permitted Uses, Prohibited Uses and Liability Limitations

Permitted Uses of Materials
The materials from this book and associated online materials are provided for educational purposes only, for the convenience of the purchasing teacher only for use in his or her lesson planning, teaching, or related educational activities. Other digital materials provided online (such as videos) are intended to be used by teachers or students to compliment the lessons provided in this book. You may use, copy, reproduce, and distribute the materials only in quantities sufficient to meet the reasonable needs of your classroom and students.

Prohibited Uses of Digital Materials
You may not sell, rent, lease, sublicense, loan, assign, time-share, or transfer, in whole or in part, any portion of this material except as stated above. You may not remove or obscure any copyright or trademark notices of Carte Diem Press as an entity of Critical Think Inc. You may not enter into any transfer or exchange of material except as provided for in herein. You may not use the digital materials provided, whether in digital or tangible form, except in conjunction with the exercises and context of this book.

You may not create any derivative works from the digital materials, except for your own noncommercial use in your classroom in conjunction with the exercises and context of this book, as provided herein.

Limitation of Carte Diem Press's Liability
As outlined in the metadata for each map document and layer package stored on ArcGIS Online, Carte Diem Press as an entity of Critical Think Inc., shall not be liable for direct, indirect, special, incidental, or consequential damages related to use of the digital materials, even if Carte Diem Press as an entity of Critical Think Inc., is advised of the possibility of such damage. Any data used is posted specifically for use with Mapping U.S. History with GIS lessons and is meant for educational purposes only.

Carte Diem Press
A division of Critical Think, Inc. 6/1/2014

ABOUT THE AUTHORS

Chris Bunin

Chris Bunin teaches Social Studies and Geospatial Technologies at Albemarle High School in Charlottesville, Virginia. He is also Assistant Professor of Geography at Piedmont Virginia Community College and the Geospatial Technologies chairperson for the Virginia Geographic Alliance. From 2006 – 2012 he worked as the Director of Teacher Scholar Programs for The Virginia Experiment and America on the World Stage Teaching American History Projects. As director, he coordinated and implemented inquiry-based experiential professional development opportunities for local history teachers.

Chris' research and instructional interests include historical geography, geospatial technologies in K-12 classrooms, and experiential education. A recipient of the National Council for Geographic Education's Distinguished Teaching Achievement Award (2006), he currently resides in Afton, Virginia with his wife, Elizabeth, son, Tucker, and daughter, Eliza.

Christine Esposito

Christine Esposito is a gifted specialist at Walker Upper Elementary School in Charlottesville City Public Schools. During her 13 years at Walker, she has taught history and language arts to fifth and sixth graders. She participated in the Virginia Experiment and America on the World Stage Teaching American History Projects (2007-2011). Her projects included Mapping the Constitutional Convention, Using Primary Sources in the Classroom, and Comparing the English Civil Wars and the American Revolution. She won the 2009 Gilder-Lehrman History Teacher of the Year award for the State of Virginia.

Her current interests include helping students to see US history within the context of world history, giving students autonomy in the classroom, medieval English history, and using Twitter (@EspoLearns) to learn from other educators. Originally from Long Island, New York, she currently resides in Charlottesville, Virginia.

CARTE DIEM PRESS
map the day

ALWAYS UP-TO-DATE

You never have to worry about the lessons "not working," because we're working hard to keep it current. **We're committed to sustainable curriculum.**

We know how fast technology changes and how important reliable curriculum is. Register your book and we will contact you when we have updated content. We'll send you a complimentary digital version of the updates.

Stay in the loop!

Register your copy today

http://gisetc.com/register